"To be honest and decisive with those who report to us, that is the call to action of *Putting the One Minute Manager to Work*."
— FRED B. RENTSCHLER, President & CEO,
Hunt-Wesson Foods, Inc., and
Swift & Company

"During the last four years, we have made the principles of *Putting the One Minute Manager to Work* a part of our management philosophy. This has made our company a better place to work and has increased sales, reduced costs and improved customer service and management retention."
— FRANK O'BRYAN, Chairman of the Board,
Shearson/American Express Mortgage Corporation

"The concepts presented in *Putting the One Minute Manager to Work* are guiding all our multi-international work force. We have taken 3,518,000 minutes (six years) to train all our managers and supervisors to become One Minute Managers. And it's making a significant difference in performance!"
— GORDON M. ANDERSON, President,
Santa Fe International Corporation

"*Putting the One Minute Manager to Work* takes off where the last book ended, and provides more excellent lessons for managers who want to be more effective."
— LOUIS P. NEEB, President,
W. R. Grace and Company,
Fast Food Division

"The uniqueness of the One Minute Manager books is their brevity, interesting style and reinforcement of proven basic management concepts. We can't be reminded too often of these, and *Putting the One Minute Manager to Work* does it so very effectively."
— ROY A. ANDERSON,
Chairman of the Board & CEO,
Lockheed Corporation

Books by Kenneth Blanchard, Ph.D.

The One Minute Manager (with Spencer Johnson), 1982

*Management of Organizational Behavior:
Utilizing Human Resources (with Paul Hersey), 4th edition,
1982*

*The Family Game: A Situational Approach to Effective
Parenting (with Paul Hersey), 1979*

*Organizational Change Through Effective Leadership (with
Robert H. Guest and Paul Hersey), 1977*

Putting

the
One
Minute
Manager

to Work

Kenneth Blanchard, Ph.D.
Robert Lorber, Ph.D.

BERKLEY BOOKS, NEW YORK

To
our wives, Margie and Sandy,
for their constant love
and support throughout
the highs and lows
of our lives.

This Berkley book contains the complete
text of the original hardcover edition.

PUTTING THE ONE MINUTE MANAGER TO WORK

A Berkley Book / published by arrangement with
William Morrow and Company, Inc.

PRINTING HISTORY
William Morrow and Company edition published 1984
Berkley trade paperback edition / May 1985

ISBN: 0-425-07757-8

A BERKLEY BOOK ® TM 757,375
Berkley Books are published by The Berkley Publishing Group,
200 Madison Avenue, New York, New York 10016.
The name "BERKLEY" and the stylized "B" with design
are trademarks belonging to Berkley Publishing Corporation.
PRINTED IN THE UNITED STATES OF AMERICA

The Symbol

The One Minute Manager's symbol—a one-minute readout from the face of a modern digital watch—is intended to remind each of us to take a minute out of our day, every now and then, to look into the faces of the people we manage. And to realize that *they* are our most important resources.

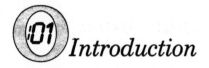 *Introduction*

In the last episode of *The One Minute Manager*, the bright young man who was searching for an effective manager learned the One Minute Manager's three secrets. He immediately realized that they were the key to effective management.

The young man learned his lessons well. Eventually he became a One Minute Manager.

He set One Minute goals.

He gave One Minute Praisings.

He delivered One Minute Reprimands.

In this second episode of *The One Minute Manager*, a veteran manager wonders whether using the three secrets on a day-to-day basis will really make a difference where it counts—in performance. He seeks the answer from a new One Minute Manager. In the process he learns how to put One Minute Management to work in a systematic way to achieve excellence.

This book is meant to be a companion to the original book. It is a practical tool that can be used independently to implement the three secrets but will probably be a richer experience if you have first read *The One Minute Manager*.

We hope you apply and use what the veteran manager learns and it makes a difference in your life and in the lives of those who work with you.

KENNETH BLANCHARD, PH.D.
ROBERT LORBER, PH.D.

01 *The One Minute Manager Library*

The response to *The One Minute Manager* which I wrote with Spencer Johnson, M.D., has been overwhelming. Being on *The New York Times* nonfiction best-seller list for over a year, selling more than a million hardback copies throughout the world, and having translations in some sixteen languages has been most satisfying. The list of men and women from major corporations as well as from fast-growing entrepreneurial companies who have found and profited from the secrets of the One Minute Manager grows daily by leaps and bounds. Our goal of writing a concise and easy-to-read book for managers—one that would make the behavioral sciences come alive for everyone who hopes to influence others—appears to have been accomplished.

The most rewarding feedback we have gotten from practicing managers is that learning would be so much easier if all management books were written in the style of *The One Minute Manager*. As a result of that universal reaction I decided to create THE ONE MINUTE MANAGER LIBRARY. My thought is to write a series of One Minute Manager books with some of the most creative and innovative management thinkers in the country. My hope is that someday a manager will be sitting at a desk wondering what the One Minute Manager has to say about a topic such as decision-making, time management, leadership, listening, delegating, team building, managing groups, and influencing upward, and all he or she will have to do is wheel around and pull from the shelf a One Minute Manager book on that subject.

To initiate the concept of a One Minute Manager Library I have teamed up with one of the outstanding consultants in the country in the area of productivity improvement, Robert Lorber, Ph.D. I decided to work with Bob because his interest in implementation and follow-up parallels my own and that of my company, Blanchard Training and Development, Inc. In fact, we work closely with his company, RL Lorber and Associates, Inc., to provide companies with the best human-resource services possible. Under Bob's direction over the last eight years, output, quality, safety, and efficiency performance-improvement programs have been initiated that have saved millions of dollars for companies throughout the world. The CEOs of a number of those companies have endorsed this book. Not only is Bob Lorber a competent professional, but he is a first-rate human being. I am proud to have worked with him on *Putting the One Minute Manager to Work*.

—KENNETH H. BLANCHARD, PH.D.

Contents

WHEN the veteran manager finished reading *The One Minute Manager*, he put the book down on his coffee table. He leaned back with a questioning look. He had first read the book at the office but had brought it home to give it another reading.

"Even after a second time through," he thought to himself, "I cannot argue with the logic of the three secrets of the One Minute Manager. But if I practice them, will I actually become a more productive manager?"

The veteran manager decided to do something about his question. The next morning he would call a manager in a town a few hours away who had, in recent years, turned a troublesome company into a very profitable enterprise. The veteran had read a newspaper interview with this manager in which he had credited much of his success to practicing One Minute Management. In fact, he now called himself a "One Minute Manager."

THE next morning when the veteran manager got to his office, he called the new One Minute Manager. He introduced himself and asked the manager if he could see him sometime that week and talk about One Minute Management. The veteran had been warned what the answer might be but he was still surprised when the One Minute Manager actually said, "Come anytime except Wednesday morning. That's when I meet with my key people. To be honest with you, I don't have much else scheduled this week. You pick the time."

"I'll be over tomorrow morning at ten," said the veteran manager, chuckling to himself. When he hung up the phone he thought, "This ought to be interesting. I'm sure I'll get my questions answered."

When the veteran manager arrived at the One Minute Manager's office, the secretary said, "He's expecting you. Go right in."

As he entered the room, he found a man in his late forties standing by the window looking out.

The veteran manager coughed and the One Minute Manager looked up. He smiled and said, "Good to see you. Let's sit down over here." He led the manager to a conversation area in the corner of the room.

"Well, what can I do for you?" the One Minute Manager asked as he sat down.

"I have read *The One Minute Manager* and so have my people," the veteran manager began. "I'm enthusiastic right now and so are they, but that has happened before when a new management system has been introduced. My question is how do you put One Minute Management to work in a way that turns the secrets into usable skills and makes a difference where it really counts—in performance?"

"Before I attempt to answer that question," said the One Minute Manager, "let me ask you one. What do you think the message of One Minute Management is?"

"It's quite simple," said the veteran manager. "If you have a sheet of paper I'll write it down for you."

The One Minute Manager went over to his desk and got a pad. He gave it to the veteran manager. Without pausing the veteran manager wrote:

*

*People Who Produce
Good Results*

*Feel Good
About Themselves*

*

"That's an interesting twist," said the One Minute Manager, gesturing to a plaque on the wall behind his desk. It read: PEOPLE WHO FEEL GOOD ABOUT THEMSELVES PRODUCE GOOD RESULTS. "Why did you change it?"

"I think it better represents the essence of One Minute Management," insisted the veteran manager, "and besides, it's more consistent with what you teach."

"Consistent?" questioned the One Minute Manager.

"Yes," responded the veteran manager firmly. "You say that one of the key ingredients to a One Minute Praising is to be specific—to tell the person exactly what he or she did right."

"That's true," said the One Minute Manager.

"Then praisings, which help make people feel good about themselves, are not effective unless those people have done something positive first," smiled the veteran manager, feeling he had the One Minute Manager trapped.

"**Y**OU'RE a tough man," laughed the One Minute Manager, "and you really have a handle on One Minute Management. I think I can learn a few things from you. I'll feel good about sharing as much as I can too."

"I doubt if you will learn much from me," said the veteran manager. "I'm just a 'street fighter' who has survived."

"Can't take a compliment, huh?" mused the One Minute Manager. "Most people can't quite accept being praised."

"I would imagine that's because we've never gotten much practice receiving praisings," said the veteran manager. "And it's not easy to do something that you're not used to doing, even if you believe in it."

"Right," said the One Minute Manager. "One of the reasons it's hard to implement One Minute Management is that people will have to change some of their old behavior. And focusing on and changing how people treat each other in organizations is something that gets only lip service. Most top managers think that management training is just a fringe benefit—a nice little frill they can give all their employees every year. That's why I have that saying on the wall," he added as he gestured to a plaque on the other side of the room. It said:

*

*Most Companies
Spend All Their Time
Looking For Another
Management Concept*

*And
Very Little Time
Following Up The One
They Have Just Taught
Their Managers*

*

"That's so true," said the veteran manager. "And people do the same thing. They're always looking for the next quick fix rather than using what they have already learned. They go from one diet program to another diet program, one exercise plan to another, without following the last program."

"Then they wonder why they don't lose weight or build up their hearts," said the One Minute Manager. "It reminds me of a story of the man who slipped and fell off a cliff while hiking on a mountaintop. Luckily he was able to grab a branch on his way down. Holding on for dear life, he looked down only to see a rock valley some fifteen hundred feet below. When he looked up it was twenty feet to the cliff where he had fallen.

"Panicked, he yelled, 'Help! Help! Is anybody up there? Help!'

"A booming voice spoke up. 'I am here and I will save you if you believe in me.'

"'I believe! I believe!' yelled back the man.

"'If you believe me,' said the voice, 'let go of the branch and then I will save you.'

"The young man, hearing what the voice said, looked down again. Seeing the rock valley below, he quickly looked back up and shouted, 'Is there anybody else up there?'"

"That's a good one," laughed the veteran manager. "That's exactly what I don't want to do—hold on to the branch and keep looking for another system. One Minute Management is the way I want to manage and be managed. All I want to know is how to put it to work so that it lasts and makes a difference."

"Then you came to the right place," said the One Minute Manager. "What problems have you been having using the three secrets?"

"I think the main difficulty I have had," said the veteran manager, "has been turning the secrets into skills. That is, knowing when to do what. For example, I think that sometimes I'm reprimanding when I should be goal setting and at other times I'm goal setting when I should be reprimanding."

"I had the same trouble," said the One Minute Manager, "until I learned my ABC's."

"I know you're not talking about the ABC's of school days," said the veteran. "So what do you mean?"

"**N**O, I'm not referring to the alphabet, but the ABC's are a way of getting back to basics. They've helped this organization make the transition from secrets to skills. We knew the three secrets of One Minute Management, and we were really enthusiastic, but they weren't influencing performance significantly until we learned the ABC's of management," said the One Minute Manager. Turning to the blackboard on his office wall he wrote:

```
A = Activators
B = Behavior
C = Consequences
```

Then he began his explanation:

"*A* stands for *activators*. Activators are those things that have to be done by a manager before someone can be expected to accomplish a goal. *B* stands for *behavior* or performance. It is what a person says or does. *C* stands for *consequences* or what a manager does after someone accomplishes or attempts to accomplish a goal. If managers can learn to understand and deliver the necessary activators (A) and consequences (C), they can ensure more productive behavior (B) or performance."

"So learning your ABC's is a good key to good performance," said the veteran.

"It certainly is," said the One Minute Manager. "A number of companies have realized that they can experience significant performance improvement by following up and getting their managers to actually use the ABC's and other implementation strategies I'll teach you."

"Could you tell me more about them?" said the veteran manager.

"I think what's interesting about these companies," said the One Minute Manager, "is that they are from a variety of businesses and industries, but in every case real bottom-line improvements were experienced. They worked on such things as productivity (both quality and quantity), safety, retention, sales, costs, and profits."

"You've got my interest," said the veteran manager. "I think I'd better learn more about the ABC's if I want to put One Minute Management to work and make those kinds of differences."

"Why don't you go see one of our people, Tom Connelly," said the One Minute Manager. "He increased retention and made major performance improvements in one of our departments. He can tell you all about the ABC's."

"I'd love to meet him," said the veteran manager. "But before you call him, let me ask you one more thing. Do you always talk in threes? First three secrets and now ABC's."

"Not always," smiled the One Minute Manager. "But I believe in the KISS method: Keep It Short and Simple. I don't think people can remember a whole lot of things, particularly if they are going to use what they have learned."

"Isn't KISS usually Keep It Simple, Stupid?" wondered the veteran manager.

"Yes," admitted the One Minute Manager. "But since One Minute Management is a positive approach to managing people, we use a positive way to express the concept."

"I knew you'd have a good explanation," smiled the veteran. "I'm looking forward to meeting Connelly."

The One Minute Manager dialed a number and said, "Tom, I have an experienced manager here who wants to learn his ABC's. Are you free?"

Although the veteran could not hear everything clearly, he smiled as he thought he heard Connelly say, "Send him over. I've just gotten back. I was out having fun catching my people doing things right."

"Stop back when you are finished talking with Tom," said the One Minute Manager as he led the veteran manager to the door.

"Sure will!" said the veteran manager. "Thanks for your time."

WHEN the veteran manager got to Connelly's office, he found a sharply dressed man in his mid-forties.

As Connelly got up from his desk and introduced himself, the veteran manager got right to the point: "Your boss told me you could give me the real lowdown on the ABC's of management."

"I'll try," said Connelly. "Let me start off by giving you this summary that we use so everyone can remember the ABC's." He handed the veteran manager a chart.

The ABC's of Management: A Summary

The term:

A	**B**	**C**
ACTIVATOR	BEHAVIOR	CONSEQUENCE

What it means:

What a manager does **before** performance	Performance: What someone says or does	What a manager does **after** performance

Examples:

One Minute Goal Setting • Areas of Accountability • Performance standards • Instructions	• Writes report • Sells product • Comes to work on time • Misses deadline • Types letter • Makes mistake • Fills order	*One Minute Praising* • Immediate, specific • Shares feelings *One Minute Reprimand* • Immediate, specific • Shares feelings • Supports individual *No Response*

The veteran manager read the chart very carefully. When he finished reading he looked up, smiled, and said, "So One Minute Goal Setting is an activator?"

"Yes," said Connelly. "An activator is like an ante in poker. It gets things started."

"If goal setting is an activator," said the veteran, "then you're not in the management game unless your people are clear on their key areas of responsibility (accountability) and what good performance in each of those areas looks like (performance standards)."

"That's why goal setting is the most important activator for managers to remember," said Connelly. "It starts the whole management process."

"Sounds good," affirmed the veteran manager. "Once people are activated, then they are ready to perform."

"They certainly are," said Connelly. "It's that performance that managers need to watch. Once you have asked someone to do something, what they say or do while trying to accomplish the desired task is their performance or behavior— the *B* of ABC's."

"Is what people think or feel considered behavior?" asked the veteran manager.

"No," said Connelly. "While thoughts and feelings are important, since they often determine what people do, they are not considered behavior because they are behind the eyeballs."

"In other words," jumped in the veteran, "you cannot see them."

"Right," said Connelly. "Once you get into thoughts and feelings, there's lots of room for complications and misunderstanding. If we stick to behavior, things are clearer because behavior can be observed and measured. As you can see from the chart, writing a report, selling a product, coming to work on time, missing a deadline, typing a letter, making a mistake, and filling an order are all behaviors."

"From that list, it seems that behavior can be either desirable or undesirable," commented the veteran manager.

"Right," said Connelly. "And how easily you are able to distinguish between the two depends on the goal-setting process. You see, if One Minute Goal Setting is done properly, the desired performance is stated in behavioral terms—that is, it can be seen (observed) and counted (measured). That is important because when you observe someone's behavior you want to be able to determine whether it is contributing toward the accomplishment of the goal (they are doing things right), or taking away from goal achievement (they are doing things wrong). That gives you an idea of how to respond as that person's boss."

"Respond?" said the veteran manager.

"Responding has to do with consequences," said Connelly. "The *C* in our ABC's. They are the responses managers give to people when they either perform a task or attempt to perform a task. Consequences follow or come after some performance."

"One Minute Praisings and One Minute Reprimands are obviously consequences," said the veteran manager.

"A One Minute Praising is an example of a positive consequence or response," said Connelly, "while a One Minute Reprimand is an example of a negative response. Whether positive or negative, the consequence has to be appropriate."

"Appropriate?" wondered the veteran manager.

"If you want people to stop doing something, give them a negative response like a One Minute Reprimand," said Connelly. "But if you want people to keep on doing something, or to improve or to learn something new, give them a positive consequence like a One Minute Praising."

"I find that using praisings and reprimands appropriately is not always easy," said the veteran manager.

"It certainly isn't," said Connelly. "One of the problems is that many managers seem to praise or reprimand their people depending on how they themselves feel on any given day, regardless of anyone's performance. If they are feeling good, they pat everyone on the back, and if they are in a bad mood, they yell at everyone."

"And I would imagine that if managers start doing that—that is, praising and reprimanding indiscriminately—their credibility will soon be shot," said the veteran manager.

"Good point," commented Connelly. "It reminds me of the story about the blind man who is walking down the street with his Seeing Eye dog. They get to a corner and while they are waiting for the light to change, the dog lifts his leg and pees on the blind man's pants. When that happens, the blind man reaches into his pocket and takes out a dog treat. Then he bends down and looks as if he is about to give it to the dog. A bystander who has seen this whole thing can't contain himself any longer so he goes up to the blind man and says, 'Sir, it's probably none of my business but I noticed that your dog took a leak on you and now you are about to give him a treat. Do you think that is really a good idea?' The blind man smiles and says, 'I'm not about to give my dog a treat. I just want to find out where his head is so I can kick him in the tail.'"

"That's beautiful," laughed the veteran. "When people see a manager isn't credible, that is confusing to them. If the blind man gave the dog a treat for inappropriate behavior like that and yelled at him when he really wasn't doing anything wrong, the dog would soon become confused and not know what to do. I have seen confusion like that in organizations. Therefore I'd better make sure I understand about consequences."

"Good idea," said Connelly.

"As I told the One Minute Manager," continued the veteran manager, "my problem is more confusion about when to be reprimanding and when to be goal setting than any difficulty between reprimanding and praising. Do you have any suggestions?"

"Yes," said Connelly. "Remember, you can effectively reprimand only winners because you can then end your negative feedback with a praising like: 'You're one of my best people—this recent performance is so unlike you.' You can't do that with people who are learning to perform and therefore have no past good performance history."

"So what do you do when people who are learning make a mistake?" queried the veteran.

"I would go back to goal setting and ante up again. You can summarize it this way," said Connelly, writing on his pad of paper:

When to Reset Goals

AND

When to Reprimand

If a person:
CAN'T DO something ——▶ Go Back to Goal Setting *(A Training Problem)*

If a person:
WON'T DO something ——▶ Reprimand *(An Attitude Problem)*

"That's very helpful," said the veteran. "So you never reprimand learners."

"No," said Connelly, "or you will immobilize them and make them even more insecure."

"So reprimands do not teach skills," observed the veteran manager. "They can just change attitudes—get skilled people back to using their abilities."

"Precisely," said Connelly. "After you reset goals with someone you are training, you don't leave that person alone. Observe the performance again and then either praise progress or go back to goal setting once more."

"It seems to me from what you're saying," commented the veteran, "that there are five steps to training a learner to be a good performer:

1. **Tell** (what to do)

2. **Show** (how to do)

Then

3. **Let** the person **try**

4. **Observe** performance

And

5. **Praise** progress
or
Redirect

"You're on the money," said Connelly. "That's a good summary of how to train someone."

"What if you keep redirecting some of your people again and again and they just don't show any progress?" questioned the veteran manager.

"You talk to such a person about career planning," laughed Connelly. "In other words, he or she just might not be in the right job."

"Given the importance of redirecting in training," said the veteran, "why don't you list it as a consequence on your ABC chart?"

"That's a good question," said Connelly. "I heard you were sharp. Redirecting certainly does follow behavior. But I never thought of it as a consequence. I'll have to add it."

"I do see from the chart, though," said the veteran, "that you have 'no response' listed as a consequence."

"It's the most popular with American managers," said Connelly. "So often managers simply ignore their people's performance, and it doesn't work."

"What do you mean?" said the veteran manager.

"What happens if you get no response after performing a task?" asked Connelly. "Your manager doesn't do or say anything."

"In the beginning, I'd try harder," said the veteran. "I'd think, 'If only I try harder maybe my boss will notice.'"

"What if your boss still doesn't notice or respond?" asked Connelly.

"After a while, I'd start doing it 'half-fast,'" smiled the veteran, getting into the humor that the One Minute Manager and his people seemed to enjoy. "Since no one seems to care whether I do this or not, why kill myself?"

"Unless you were doing something that was motivating to you in and of itself," said Connelly.

"If that occurred you would be confused about the difference between work and play," said the veteran manager.

"That's an interesting way to put it," said Connelly. "If you are doing what you enjoy at work, you will continue to do it well regardless of whether anyone notices and pats you on the back. But generally, no response to good performance, like a negative consequence, tends to decrease the possibility of that performance being repeated."

"Let me see if I have all this straight," said the veteran manager as he showed Connelly his notes:

*

Only
Positive
Consequences

Encourage
Good
Future
Performance

*

"That's the headline," said Connelly, "and yet, what are the most frequent responses managers give to the performance of their people?"

"Negative or no response at all," said the veteran manager. "As we both know, the American way of managing seems to be: When people perform well, their managers do nothing. When they make a mistake, their managers 'hit' them."

"It's the old 'leave alone-zap' technique," said Connelly with a smile. "Not a very effective way of motivating people."

"But a very easy habit to fall into," said the veteran manager. "I've done it myself. I can see now that if I'm going to manage my people, I'd better learn to manage consequences."

"That's an important lesson to learn," said Connelly. "Most people think that activators have a greater influence on performance than consequences. And yet, only fifteen to twenty-five percent of what influences performance comes from activators like goal setting, while seventy-five to eighty-five percent of it comes from consequences like praisings and reprimands."

"You're saying that what happens after a person does something has more impact than what happens before?" questioned the veteran skeptically.

"That's it," said Connelly. "Performance is determined mainly by consequences. That's why the One Minute Manager is so vehement about the importance of follow-up. We believe you should spend ten times as much time following up your management training as it took to plan and conduct an initial program. Otherwise people will revert back to old behavior within a short period."

"Yes, but if you don't set goals, the chances are low that people will do what you want them to do in the first place," interjected the veteran manager.

"Right," said Connelly. "But all the goal setting in the world without any managing of consequences—praising good performance and reprimanding poor—will only get things started and provide short-term success for a manager. In other words, managers will get the performance they want only when they are there, but when they are not there, people may or may not engage in the behavior the manager wants. We have a saying that emphasizes the importance of managing consequences," said Connelly as he pointed to a plaque on the wall.

*

As A Manager
The Important Thing
Is Not What Happens
When You Are There

But
What Happens When
You Are Not There

*

"That's so true," said the veteran. "I can always get the performance I want from people, even from my kids at home, when I am there. But I'm not around all the time. In fact, I think I spend as much, if not more, time at work with my peers (at the same level in the organization) and with my boss as I do with my subordinates."

"So the way you can really tell how good a manager you are," said Connelly, "is not by what happens when you are there, but by what happens when you're not there. And the secret to getting good performance from your people when you're *not* there is how effectively you deliver consequences when you *are* there—both praisings and reprimands."

"It is clear to me now," said the veteran manager, "what you meant when you said activators are important for starting good performance—getting it done the first time—but what really determines and influences whether that desired performance will be repeated when you are not there is what happens after the original performance. The 'leave alone-zap' approach just frustrates and alienates people."

"The whole purpose of teaching our people their ABC's," said Connelly, "is to ensure that they sequence One Minute Goal Setting, One Minute Praisings, and One Minute Reprimands in the proper order. It's a behavioral reminder."

"You have certainly shown me how to begin to turn the secrets into skills," said the veteran. "I don't think I'll ever forget when to do what anymore. But let me ask one more question. You have been emphasizing the importance of clear, good goal setting, followed by One Minute Praisings for good performance. I seem to have lost the idea of the effective use of One Minute Reprimands. Could you share with me some of the positive uses of reprimands again?"

"You might want to talk to the One Minute Manager about the effective use of One Minute Reprimands," said Connelly. "He loves to teach that secret, and besides, he would be willing to answer any questions you have about One Minute Goal Setting and One Minute Praisings as well."

"That's a good idea," said the veteran manager. "I certainly have taken up enough of your time."

"That's OK," said Connelly. "I have enjoyed it. Besides, knowing my ABC's has really helped me free up a lot of my time."

"I hope it does the same for me," said the veteran.

A S the veteran manager left Connelly's office, he found his mind going a mile a minute. Connelly had been quite helpful. As he approached the One Minute Manager's office, the manager's secretary smiled. "Did you have a good meeting with Tom Connelly?" she asked.

"I sure did," the veteran manager replied, returning her smile. "Could I see the boss?"

"Go right in," she said. "He was wondering if you were coming back."

As the veteran entered the office, he found the One Minute Manager looking out his favorite window. He turned as he heard the veteran manager enter.

"You were with Connelly for quite a while. The two of you must have gotten along quite well," he said.

"It was most helpful," said the veteran. "But I have some concerns about the use of reprimands," he went on. "In teaching me the ABC's, Connelly seemed to stress the importance of praisings but downplayed the use of reprimands. I know you believe in delivering bad news sometimes. Maybe I just need some reorientation."

"The best way for me to respond to your concerns about reprimanding," replied the One Minute Manager, "is to start by talking about managing winners—people with proven track records. Winners are easy to supervise. All you have to do is ante up One Minute Goals and then they are off."

"That fits with my experience," said the veteran manager. "While everyone likes a pat on the back once in a while, you don't have to praise winners very much. They usually beat you to the punch. Besides not praising winners very much, you don't often have to reprimand them either, do you?"

"No!" said the One Minute Manager. "Good performers are usually self-correcting. If they make a mistake, they fix it before anyone else notices."

"But everyone makes a mistake sometimes that he or she is unaware of," stated the veteran manager.

"Then you may have to reprimand," said the One Minute Manager. "However, if they know the three secrets, good performers don't resent it because of the way you deliver that reprimand."

"I assume you are talking about ending the reprimand with a praising," commented the veteran manager.

"Precisely," said the One Minute Manager.

"Connelly cleared up for me why you don't reprimand a learner, but I still have trouble understanding why you praise someone at the end of a reprimand," said the veteran manager.

"Remember, you only reprimand when you know the person can do better," the One Minute Manager reminded him. "When you leave your people after a reprimand, you want them to be thinking about what they did wrong, not about the way you treated them."

"I don't understand," the veteran hesitated.

"LET me see if I can explain it this way," said the One Minute Manager. "Most people not only don't end their reprimands with a praising, they give the person a parting shot: 'If you think you're going to get promoted, you have another think coming.' Now when you leave that person, especially if there is a co-worker within earshot, what do you think these folks will be talking about? How you treated the person you were reprimanding or what the person did wrong?"

"How you treated the person," said the veteran manager.

"Precisely," said the One Minute Manager. "They're talking about what an SOB you are. And yet that person did something wrong. If you end your reprimand with a praising, you will be telling the person, 'You are OK but your behavior isn't!' Then when you leave, the person will be thinking about what he or she did wrong. If for any reason he tries to badmouth you to co-workers, they will stop it by saying, 'What are you getting so excited about? He said you were one of his best people. He just doesn't want you to make that mistake again.'"

"I think I understand what you're saying about ending with a praising," said the veteran manager. "See if this is a good summary comment." He showed his notes to the One Minute Manager. They said:

*

*When You
End A Reprimand
With A Praising*

*People Think
About
Their Behavior
Not
Your Behavior*

*

"That's very well put," said the One Minute Manager. "I'm reminded of a personal experience I had that proves your point. One Friday night my wife said to me, 'Great manager of people . . .' Whenever she says that I know our kids have done something wrong and I am about to get the problem dumped in my lap. She had just caught Karen [our fifteen-year-old daughter] sneaking out of the house with a bottle of vodka on the way to the football game.

"'I think I will kill her,' said my wife. 'Could you take over?'

"I have a lot of respect for single parents because there is no one in the bullpen they can call on. We have always had a strategy: If one of us is out of control, we throw the ball to the other.

"Since I had just learned about the reprimand, I thought this might be a good opportunity to see if it worked. I said, 'Where is Karen?' My wife said, 'She's in the kitchen.' So I went right out to the kitchen and found Karen standing there looking like she was about to be sent to the dungeon. I walked right up to her and put my hand gently on her shoulder. I said, 'Karen, Mom tells me she just caught you sneaking out of the house with a bottle of vodka. Let me tell you how I feel about that. I can't believe it. How many times have I told you the way kids get killed is to have some kid drinking and driving. And to be sneaking around with a bottle of vodka . . .'

"Now I knew that the rule of the reprimand was that you only have about thirty seconds to share your feelings."

"I bet you wanted two hours," said the veteran.

"You better believe it," laughed the One Minute Manager. "Some parents take a whole weekend. Your child does something wrong on Friday night and you chew the kid out. A half hour later you see the same kid and you say, 'Let me tell you one other thing. . . .' Then you see the kid the next morning and you say, 'Let me tell you about your friends too. . . .' You spend the whole weekend making everyone miserable over one misbehavior.

"The rule about the reprimand is that you only have thirty seconds to share your feelings, and when it's over—it's over. Don't keep beating on the person for the same mistake.

"Recognizing all this, I had to come to a screeching halt in sharing my feelings with Karen. It was at this point that I realized the importance of pausing for a moment of silence in between sharing your feelings and the last part of the reprimand. It permits you to calm down and at the same time lets the person you are reprimanding feel the intensity of your feelings. So I took a deep breath while Karen was swallowing hard. Then I said, 'Let me tell you one other thing, Karen. I love you. You're a real responsible kid. Mom and I normally don't have to worry about you. This sounds like some other kid. You're better than that. That's why Mom and I are not going to let you get away with that kind of behavior.'

"Then I gave her a hug and said, 'Now get off to the game but remember, you're better than that.'"

"I'm not sure I would have let her go to the game after something like that," said the veteran. "I bet she couldn't believe it herself."

"She couldn't believe it," confirmed the One Minute Manager. "But I told her, 'Now you know how I feel about teenage drinking and sneaking around. I know you're not going to do that again, so have a good time.'

"In the past, before I knew about the One Minute Reprimand, not only would I not have ended her reprimand with a praising, I would have sent her to her room, screaming something like 'You're not going to another football game until you're twenty-five.'

"Now, if I had sent her to her room, what do you think she would have been thinking about? What she did wrong or how I had treated her?" asked the One Minute Manager.

"How you had treated her," said the veteran manager. "I bet she would have been on the phone immediately, telling her friends what a monster you were. Teenagers love to share parent stories."

"Absolutely," said the One Minute Manager. "And then she would have been psychologically off the hook for what she had done wrong, with all her attention focused on how I had treated her."

"What happened next?" asked the veteran, feeling he was in the middle of a soap opera.

"The next morning," continued the One Minute Manager, "when I was eating breakfast, Karen came downstairs. Wondering how I had done, I asked her, 'Karen, how did you like the way I dealt with the vodka incident last night?'

"'I hated it,' she said. 'You ruined the football game for me.'

"'I ruined the football game for you?'

"'Yes,' she said. 'Because all through the game I kept thinking about what I had done and how much I had disappointed you and Mom!'

"I smiled to myself and thought, 'It worked! It really worked! She was concentrating on what she had done wrong and not on how I had treated her.'"

"That was a very helpful, clear example," said the veteran manager. "I think I've got that part of the reprimand, but I'd like to ask you a couple more things about the One Minute Reprimand."

"Fire away," said the One Minute Manager. "Most of the questions we get about One Minute Management have to do with the reprimand."

"What if the person you are reprimanding—Karen, for example—starts to argue with you?" asked the veteran.

"You stop what you are saying right then," said the One Minute Manager, "and make it very clear to that person that this is not a discussion. 'I am sharing my feelings about what you did wrong, and if you want to discuss it later, I will. But for right now this is not a two-way discussion. I am telling you how I feel.'"

"That's helpful," said the veteran. "One other thing. If I buy praising someone at the end of a reprimand, why not begin a reprimand with a praising? When I did reprimands in the past, I used the 'sandwich approach': Pat 'em on the back, kick 'em in the butt, pat 'em on the back."

"I know that style well," said the One Minute Manager, "but I've learned that it is very important to keep praisings and reprimands separate. If you start a reprimand with a praising, then you will ruin the impact of your praising."

"Why?" asked the veteran manager.

"Because when you go to see a person just to praise him," said the One Minute Manager, "he will not hear your praising because he will be wondering when the other shoe will drop—what bad news will follow the good."

"So by keeping praisings and reprimands in order, you will let your people hear both more clearly," summarized the veteran. "What about more tangible punishments like demotion, being transferred, or some other penalty? Are they ever appropriate?"

"Our experience with the One Minute Reprimand," said the One Minute Manager, "suggests that you usually do not need to add some additional penalty. It is an uncomfortable enough experience."

"That was beautifully illustrated with Karen," said the veteran manager. "I think you really cleared up my questions about reprimands. And also, I can now see how learning the ABC's helps managers take their knowledge of One Minute Management and translate it into action. But how can you integrate One Minute Management into a total organizational program for performance improvement?"

"You have to pay the PRICE," said the One Minute Manager with a smile.

"What is PRICE?" asked the veteran manager.

"The PRICE system," said the One Minute Manager, "goes beyond the ABC's by providing managers with five easy-to-follow steps that can involve everyone in improving performance."

"It sounds fascinating," said the veteran, "but my head is already swimming from all that I have learned today."

"Why don't you stay overnight locally and we can get together at nine in the morning? I'll ask my secretary to make a reservation for you at the Osborn Hotel. The manager there is really excited about One Minute Management and has implemented a unique praising program designed to catch his employees doing things right. I think you will find it most interesting."

"Sounds good to me," said the veteran.

WHEN the veteran manager arrived at the hotel, he went straight to the registration desk. As he was checking in, the receptionist said, "Our customers are important to us. I wonder if I can ask you to do us a favor during your visit."

"Sure," said the veteran. "What is it?"

"We'd like you to take this book of 'praising coupons.'* If any of our employees treats you the way you like to be treated, would you tear off a coupon, write on the back what the employee did right, find out what his or her name is, and turn it in at the manager's office?"

"So all your customers are catching your employees doing things right," laughed the veteran. "I bet a praising comes with each coupon the manager receives."

"You read the Book," exclaimed the receptionist with a smile.

"I did. Your hotel really seems to be putting One Minute Management to work," said the veteran.

"It's a fantastic system!" responded the receptionist enthusiastically. "Have a nice evening."

---

*Drew Dimond, former district director of Holiday Inns, Inc., in Nashville, Tennessee, got excited about *The One Minute Manager* and decided to implement a praising-coupon program in one of his hotels. Gary Wood, the hotel manager, ran with the ball. The results described here are similar to those they have observed in this Holiday Inn.

After an early dinner, the veteran went straight to his room to relax. He was amazed by how well he had been treated by all the hotel employees. He had already given out three coupons—to the bellman, his waitress, and the maitre d'. Catching people doing things right was changing his whole attitude toward this hotel. The praising coupons made it his job as a guest not to complain but to compliment.

The next morning, the veteran manager packed his bags and headed downstairs. After having breakfast he checked out. On his way out of the hotel, he stopped by the manager's office to drop off his praising coupons. The manager happened to be there.

As he handed the manager his praising coupons, the veteran manager said, "I think this praising program of yours is a great idea. It's a very practical way to put One Minute Management to work. Have there been any tangible bottom-line effects of the program?"

"While we have only had the system in place for about five months," said the hotel manager, "we have already seen significant reductions in absenteeism and turnover. Our employees look forward to coming to work now because they are anxious to see if they can be caught doing something right. And we have not been giving any financial payoffs for coupons—just a pat on the back for a job well done."

"Do you think this program has changed the customers' attitudes, too?" wondered the veteran.

"Absolutely!" said the hotel manager. "Our greatest improvement has been in guest inspection scores. Our guests are asked to rate the hotel on an ABCDF scale on such items as value/cost, appearance, service, and friendliness. Prior to the praising program fewer than seventy percent of the guests who filled out the guest inspections cards rated the hotel in the A to B range. After the first five months of the program, the scores are averaging over ninety percent A's and B's and we are getting three times as many returned cards."

"So your praising coupons are paying high dividends for you, your customers, and your employees," said the veteran manager.

"Yes," said the hotel manager. "Putting the One Minute Manager to work pays a good return on investment."

As the veteran manager shook hands with the hotel manager, he smiled and said, "My stay here has been very profitable to me too!"

WHEN the veteran arrived at the One Minute Manager's office, he found him in his usual pose by the window. When he sensed the veteran standing in the doorway, the One Minute Manager turned around and greeted him with a friendly handshake and offered the veteran a chair at the conference table.

"Well, did you enjoy your stay at the Osborn Hotel last night?" the One Minute Manager asked as he sat down.

"I certainly did," responded the veteran, "and you were right—it was unique!"

"I wanted you to experience," confided the One Minute Manager, "an attempt to put One Minute Management to work before we talked today. I thought it would help you understand our PRICE system better."

As the veteran manager was listening to the One Minute Manager, he noticed a new plaque on his desk. It read:

*

Don't Just Do Something—

Sit There

*

The veteran manager smiled because he knew how the usual frantic, yet inefficient, pace of most organizations demanded the opposite.

"My key people gave it to me," said the One Minute Manager, when he saw the veteran looking at the plaque. "They thought it symbolized the importance of goal setting as a means of avoiding the 'activity trap.'"

"The activity trap?" wondered the veteran manager.

"That's where people are running around trying to do things right before anyone has stopped to figure out the right things to do."

"Talking about doing things right," said the veteran, "What's the best way for me to learn PRICE?"

"Why don't you go and talk to Alice Smith," suggested the One Minute Manager. "She's one of our most creative managers. She helped us develop the PRICE system. Since she took over our sales operation, sales have skyrocketed."

As the One Minute Manager was calling Alice Smith, the veteran manager was smiling to himself. He thought, "They certainly have taken all the mystique out of managing people. I'll bet PRICE is really quite simple, but powerful."

"Well, Alice is all set to see you," said the One Minute Manager. "You can head over to her office right away. She is in the same building as Connelly but on the third floor."

WHEN the veteran manager got to Alice Smith's office, he found her working quietly at her desk. He thought to himself, "At last a One Minute Manager who seems to be doing some work."

She smiled as he entered. "So you want to know if the PRICE is right," she said as she beckoned the veteran to sit down.

"Corny but true," said the veteran. "I'm anxious to get started."

"That's important because the PRICE system is the nuts and bolts of how to put the One Minute Manager to work and make a difference every day in the performance and satisfaction of people on the job. But you have to listen carefully because now we take the three basic skills and turn them into five important steps."

Smith immediately went to the small blackboard behind her desk and wrote:

Pinpoint
Record
Involve
Coach
Evaluate

"**P**INPOINT is the process of defining key performance areas for people in observable, measurable terms," began Smith. "In essence, it is the performance areas that you would identify as One Minute Goals."

"Suppose I told you I was concerned about my work group," said the veteran manager, "and I wanted to rekindle commitment from my people. Would that be specific enough?"

"No," said Smith. "We can't improve morale, poor attitude, laziness, or things like that without more information."

"Isn't it important to deal with morale problems in organizations?" asked the veteran manager.

"Sure it is, but I would have to pinpoint what you mean by poor morale," explained Smith. "Do you mean people are coming to work late, or quality rejects are frequent, or people are bickering at work? What do you mean by poor morale?"

"So we need to stop managers from saying things are good or bad," said the veteran, "and get them to identify specifically what is happening."

"That's what pinpointing is all about," said Smith, pleased by the veteran's ability to learn quickly. "Establishing the areas you are going to measure and how you are going to measure them—for example, in quantity, quality, cost (on or off budget), or timeliness."

"Where does that bring us?" interrupted the veteran.

"**D**IRECT to RECORD," answered Smith. "Once you have pinpointed an area for improvement or a One Minute Goal, you want to be able to measure present performance and track progress in that area. You will notice I talk about areas that you want to improve, not problems. People have trouble admitting there are problems, but everyone has an area he or she would like to improve."

"You mean you would gather actual data on how often people are late to work, how frequently products are rejected because of quality, and the like?" asked the veteran.

"That's right," said Smith. "You want to take the guesswork out of performance improvement."

"What if someone says, 'You can't measure performance in my job!'" wondered the veteran manager.

"When a person tells us that," said Smith, "we suggest that maybe we should eliminate the position and see if we've lost anything. It's amazing how interested they suddenly get in establishing ways to identify goals and measure performance in their jobs."

"Could you give me an example," said the veteran, "of a performance-improvement area you ran through the PRICE system?"

"Yes," said Smith. "When I took over the department, the old sales manager told me, 'Phone contact needs improvement around here. Salespeople never make appointments with customers by phone. They think they have to be on the road all the time. When they get to the customer, he's often out for the morning, or he's busy and can't be interrupted. They have to wait to see him so they end up spending all their time in coffee shops. If they made appointments, they'd get twice as much done in half the time.'

"I asked, 'How do you know phone contact needs improvement?'

"'I just feel everything starts there,' he replied. 'That's always been an issue in this company.'

"Then I asked, 'Have you counted it? Is there any way to tell exactly the number of phone calls salespeople make to customers?'

"'Well,' he said, 'I could check their phone logs. Each salesperson is required to keep a daily log of calls right by his or her phone.'

"When I put a count to it, I found that making appointments was not a crucial issue for everyone. In fact, only three salespeople were delinquent in their phoning," Smith stated.

"By recording or measuring performance," said the veteran, "you attempt to make sure the need for improvement is real and not just a feeling. You don't want to 'fix what ain't broken.'"

"Precisely," said Smith. "It's most effective to plot the information on a graph," she explained as she pulled a folder from her desk file. "Here's an initial graph I made of appointment calls for one of my salespeople, Jack.

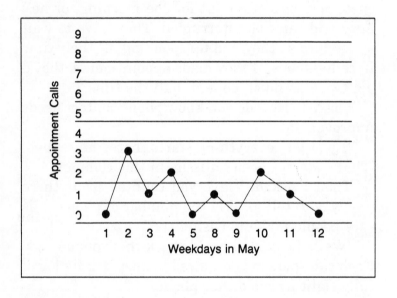

"On any of the graphs we use, we put time across the bottom or horizontal axis, and the pinpointed behavior along the side or the vertical axis," explained Smith. "The time element for Jack was weekdays in May for a two-week period and the behavior was the number of appointment calls made each day.

"**A**FTER I made the graph I calculated Jack's mean number of daily appointment calls. Over two weeks, he averaged one call a day. I knew improvement was needed since there was a difference between actual performance and what I thought was desired performance. I was ready for the INVOLVE step in PRICE."

"Is that when you informed Jack about his performance problem?" questioned the veteran.

"Yes," said Smith. "Once you are aware improvement is needed, you share that information with whoever is responsible (accountable) for that area and/or can influence performance in it—in our example it would be Jack."

"I bet when you've graphed all this performance data on Jack and it shows clearly that he is not doing what you think he should be doing, there's a real temptation to let Jack have it," observed the veteran. "Give him the old 'leave alone-zap.'"

"There often is," said Smith, "but you need to control yourself. The time for reprimanding hasn't come yet. In fact, it is important to remember that graphs are not meant to be used as weapons, or as evidence in a managerial prosecution. They are designed to be used as training tools as well as nonjudgmental methods of feedback."

"So how do you share your graph with Jack?"

"Without judgment," said Smith. "And in a spirit of learning. You want Jack to learn, and you assume that Jack wants to improve. You know the saying around here:

*

*Feedback
Is The
Breakfast
Of
Champions*

*

"How true that is," affirmed the veteran. "But tell me, how do you involve someone like Jack besides giving him feedback on results?"

"You involve him in establishing the activators," said Smith. "That is, in deciding what has to be agreed upon before Jack can be expected to improve his performance to the desired level."

"Besides goal setting, what other agreements do you have to ante up?" smiled the veteran, enjoying the opportunity to show off what he had already learned.

"Coaching and evaluation strategies," answered Smith. "You need to agree about how you are going to supervise Jack as well as how he will be evaluated and what payoff he can anticipate for improved performance."

"Do you always involve your people in establishing One Minute Goals?" wondered the veteran manager.

"Yes, in most cases," said Smith. "*One Minute Management just doesn't work unless you share it with your people.* Otherwise they will think you are trying to manipulate them. That is particularly true with goal setting. Shared goal setting tends to get greater commitment from people and guarantees the setting of a realistic goal for the performance area."

"A realistic goal?" puzzled the veteran manager.

"A realistic goal is moderately difficult but achievable," explained Smith. "It's acceptable to you as a manager and it's possible for your people to accomplish. Let's go back to Jack. He has been setting up one appointment a day by phone. How many appointment calls are acceptable to you? How many are attainable by Jack?"

"How many does the best salesperson make?" inquired the veteran manager.

"Comparing Jack to the best won't encourage him. It will only discourage him," answered Smith. "Remember, we're using this method as a training tool, not as a punishment."

"What goal would you set?" asked the veteran, shrugging his shoulders.

"I'd probably say, 'Jack, let's see if you can make three appointment calls a day next week. How does that sound?'"

"So you have to be specific about the number and the time frame," commented the veteran.

"Exactly," said Smith. "What do you suppose would happen if I simply said to Jack, 'I'd like you to make more appointment calls. I don't think you have been making enough lately'?"

"He'd probably say OK," said the veteran, "and then not take it seriously."

"That's why I'd make a graph with Jack by my side," said Smith. "Then he'd know I was serious and know exactly what he had to do to get back into my good graces."

She removed another graph from the file she had gotten from her desk. "This was Jack's first goal-setting graph," said Smith as she handed the veteran the graph.

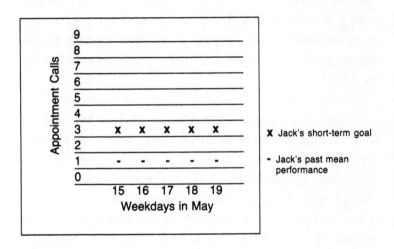

"You see, we plotted Jack's past mean performance (one call a day) and his short-term goal (three calls a day). That way he could see the difference between where he'd been and where he was headed," explained Smith.

"Why wouldn't you say you wanted Jack to make an appointment call for every sales visit he was going to make?" wondered the veteran.

"That might have been an appropriate goal in the long run," said Smith, "but in the short run you couldn't expect that kind of turnaround in behavior because Jack had obviously gotten himself into some bad work patterns. Just as you can't expect to lose twenty-five pounds today, but you do want some change. So we had to set a short-term goal with Jack, like three appointment calls a day."

"Short-term goal?" wondered the veteran.

"It's a first step," said Smith. "When you set up a performance-improvement program with people, remember not to set the end-result goal (in this case an appointment call for *every* sales visit— about six or seven calls per workday) as the goal that has to be reached before someone can feel a sense of accomplishment and deserve a praising; otherwise you might have to wait forever."

"I remember that concept now," said the veteran. "In the beginning, when working on performance, you need to set things up so you can catch people doing things approximately right (short-term goal), not exactly right (final goal)."

"Precisely," said Smith. "The journey to exactly right is make up of a whole series of approximately rights."

"So Rome can't be built in a day," said the veteran. "As a result, what you want to do is keep track of progress from present performance to the desired level. What's the best way to do that?"

"By involving people in coaching," said Smith. "As you know, once people are clear on what they are being asked to do, coaching is essentially observing their performance and giving them feedback on results. But the whole coaching process is set up by agreeing ahead of time with your people when and how you are going to give them feedback. That part of coaching is done during the Involve step."

"I would imagine," interrupted the veteran, "that by designing, with your people, the feedback system you are going to use, you are increasing the chances of their winning—accomplishing their goals."

"Exactly," said Smith. "Setting up a good feedback system through performance graphs is crucial if you hope to do any day-to-day coaching. That's why, with Jack, we agreed that for the first week I'd stop by his desk every day and review his phone log. I'd graph his performance and share it with him."

"What other coaching agreements did you make besides your daily visits?" asked the manager.

"Recording performance every day can be time-consuming," said Smith. "So we agreed to meet again after the first week to evaluate when Jack could begin to administer his own feedback."

"Administer his own feedback?" repeated the veteran.

"If I am having a performance problem with Jack, what I want to do is set up a graph that Jack is able to use. He can put his own check marks, stars, or whatever on the graph."

"Then he's able to say, 'Hey, I'm doing better,' or 'I'm doing worse,'" suggested the veteran manager. "He can even begin to praise or reprimand himself."

"Yes," said Smith. "Feedback that is self-administered can be immediate—as close to the performance as possible."

"At this point, what else did you involve Jack in?" asked the veteran.

"All I had left to do in the 'I' step in the PRICE system was to involve Jack in performance evaluation," said Smith.

"How did you intend to do that?" asked the veteran manager.

"When we set up the graph, Jack knew how his performance was going to be evaluated, but to complete his involvement in performance evaluation, we still had to decide what was in it for Jack if he improved," said Smith.

"What do you mean?" asked the veteran.

"What positive consequence will happen for Jack if he reaches his goal," Smith answered.

"Did I hear you say that you and Jack had to decide together? Didn't you just tell him?" responded the veteran.

"If Jack had been less capable and committed, I would have determined the rewards. But Jack knew best what rewards would motivate him," explained Smith. "I asked Jack, 'What will motivate you to make more calls?' He said, 'If I make my quota, write me a note. I collect those things. I have every letter of commendation I've received since high school. But don't have your secretary type me some form letter. Write it by hand.'

"I thought that was a great idea. I said, 'What if you don't meet your quota?' He said, 'Come and tell me I deserve a reprimand. You probably won't even have to deliver it. But just knowing that you know I am slipping back to old behavior will get me back on track.'"

"Did you keep track of the praisings versus the number of reprimands?" laughed the veteran.

"It might sound funny," said Smith, "but I did exactly that. I started a log of praisings and reprimands. It worked beautifully. Now I keep a praising/reprimand log* on all my employees. It's just a list of names with *P*'s and *R*'s after each name with a shorthand note about what happened. It keeps me on track with One Minute Management."

---

*Ted Fletcher, manager, training and development, for the Nestlé Company, shared One Minute Management with one of his division managers, Ed Dippold. Now they are keeping praising and reprimand logs on each of their people in their New Jersey plant. Ed reports, "It really works! With union employees and foremen who rotate on shifts, it has kept communications clear and open."

"THAT makes sense," said the veteran manager. "So prior to actually coaching or evaluating performance, the consequences for goal accomplishment have to be agreed upon in the Involve (I) step of the PRICE system."

"In Jack's case," said Smith, "he knew what the goals (short- and long-term) were, how I was going to supervise or coach him, and how his performance would be evaluated, including the consequences he could expect for poor performance as well as for improved performance."

"Now that all those things were settled," interrupted the veteran, "Jack was ready to start improving his appointment-call behavior."

"Yes," said Smith. "And at that point, my role changed from involving Jack in decision making about establishing the necessary activators to observing his performance and managing the consequences."

"That's what coaching is all about," said the veteran. "Observing behavior and giving feedback on results—both praisings and reprimands. And that's when you began the 'C' or COACH step in PRICE."

"You've got it. Now I can show you how well Jack did," said Smith. "Here's his graph from the first week."

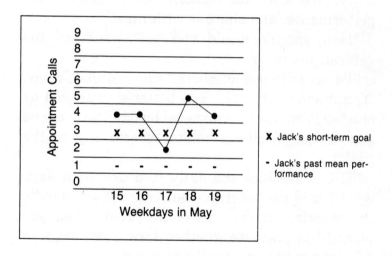

X Jack's short-term goal

- Jack's past mean performance

"That's great. He bettered his goal except on the third day," commented the veteran manager as he read the graph. "When did you tell him about his improvement, at your planned meeting at the end of the week?"

"Absolutely not," said Smith. "Remember a basic rule of feedback is that it should be immediate and specific. If the data flow is vague and delayed, it is not an effective training tool. And besides I had made an agreement with Jack that during the first week I'd stop by his desk daily, review his phone log, graph his performance, and share it with him."

"How specific would you be?" wondered the veteran manager.

"I'd actually use numbers," said Smith. "I'd say, 'You made your goal,' 'You bettered your goal by one,' or 'You missed your goal by one.' So once the goal is set, feedback relates specifically to the goal."

"OK. I see how the daily feedback with Jack went," said the veteran, "but how did you handle the meeting at the end of the week when you planned to evaluate whether Jack could begin to administer his own feedback or not?"

"I was happy with Jack's progress that first week," said Smith, "so I was willing to listen to any suggestions he might have about how I should monitor his performance and give him feedback. Remember, as people improve, you want to gradually turn over to them more and more of the responsibility for monitoring their own performance.

"Jack was very aware of his needs," observed Smith proudly. "He said, 'Look, if you leave me entirely alone, I'm going to feel abandoned. But I don't want you coming to my desk every day. It makes me nervous. For the next month let me do the daily graph myself and you come by on Fridays to check it out. If I need some help during the week, I'll come see you.'"

"So you worked out a new agreement with him," said the veteran. "Did you keep doing that until he performed like a winner in that part of his job?"

"Absolutely," said Smith. "I want to supervise my people closely only if they need it. As soon as they can perform on their own, I am ready to let go. In coaching you want to schedule fewer and fewer feedback meetings as people move gradually from their present level of performance to the desired level of performance. We have an expression that we use here that I think would be important for you to learn." She wrote on her pad:

*

*Achieving
Good Performance
Is
A Journey—
Not
A Destination*

*

"**T**HAT'S well put," said the veteran. "Many managers just shout out destinations (goals) and then sit back and wait for people to reach them. What's helpful about the PRICE system is that it suggests that coaching is a process of managing the journey. I'm ready to move on to EVALUATE (E), the last step in the PRICE system. Are you?"

"Why not?" said Smith. "After all, evaluation and coaching go hand in hand. In fact, every time you give someone feedback you are evaluating. You want to continually determine how well performance is going in pinpointed areas. Are you getting the results you want? If not, why not?"

"If evaluation and coaching go hand in hand," said the veteran manager, "why do you have Evaluate as a separate step in the PRICE system?"

"Because most organizations have actual formal performance-review sessions," said Smith. "These sessions are held quarterly, semiannually, or only once a year. In the PRICE system we recommend that you graph and track performance in pinpointed One Minute goal areas for no longer than six weeks without having a formal evaluation session. Unless the person is a proven winner."

"What do you discuss in these sessions?" wondered the veteran.

"Nothing new," said Smith. "All we do is review what we have been talking about throughout the coaching progress. "It is a way to formally recognize progress and a time to evaluate future strategies. Can the manager turn over the supervision of the PRICE project(s) to the people involved or is direction and help still needed?"

"While evaluation in the PRICE system is a continuous process," said the veteran, "I don't get the feeling it is a punitive process. A One Minute Manager does not try to trip people up."

"David Berlo, one of the most thoughtful teachers and consultants I have ever met," said Smith, "gave me the best expression of that philosophy. He got interested in the training of whales. One day he asked some of his training friends in Florida whether they actually trained the whales by using some of the concepts we have been talking about in the coaching process. They said, 'Yes, with one addition.'"

"What was that?" wondered the veteran.

"Before they attempted to train the whales to do anything," said Smith, "the trainers told David, 'We feed them and make sure they're not hungry. And then we jump in the water and play with the whales until we have convinced them . . .'"

"Convinced them of what?" wondered the veteran manager.

"Let me write that down for you," said Smith, "because it underlies everything that One Minute Management stands for." She reached over and borrowed the veteran manager's note pad and began to write.

*

We
Mean
Them
No
Harm

*

"That's a powerful statement," said the veteran manager as he read what Alice Smith had written. "That's all about trust, isn't it?"

"It sure is," said Smith. "David is writing a book entitled *I Mean You No Harm* because he feels that most of the performance review and evaluation systems that companies set up in our country suggest the very opposite."

"Now that you mention it," said the veteran, "that is so true. Most evaluation systems suggest that there always have to be winners and losers."

"That's just not part of the philosophy of the One Minute Manager," said Smith.

"So, when you talk about evaluation in the PRICE system," said the veteran, "you are always trying to find out whether you are getting the desired results. If you are, your people get recognized and praised. And if you're not, they get redirected or reprimanded depending on whether the problem is one of ability or motivation. Are there any other reasons why you wouldn't be getting the desired results?"

"Performance can break down at every step of the PRICE system," responded Smith. "You might have pinpointed an irrelevant area. Or you might be recording data ineffectively. In involving your people you might have agreed upon too low or too high a goal, your feedback might be erratic, or your consequences not sufficiently motivating."

"So you are taking some significant responsibility for ensuring that your people perform well," said the veteran manager.

"Most definitely," said Smith. "My job as a manager is not just to sit back, cross my arms, look stern, and evaluate. It's to roll up my sleeves and be responsive to people and what they need to perform well."

"So you have to keep your eyes and ears open," interjected the veteran. "I would imagine you often go back to Pinpoint and start the process again. So PRICE is a continuous process."

"Exactly," said Smith. "That's why we like to show PRICE almost like a dial on the telephone." She pointed to a plaque on the wall. It read:

Putting the One Minute Manager to Work

A Summary of the
PRICE SYSTEM

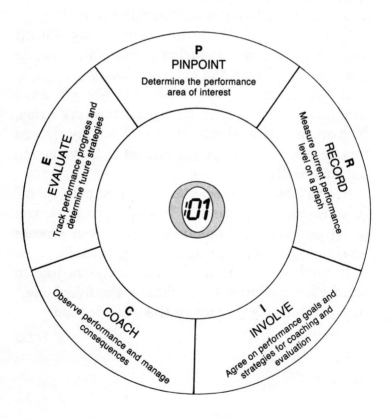

"THAT'S great. Now I can dial *P* for *performance,*" said the veteran with a smile.

"Let me emphasize one last thing about PRICE," said Smith. "You can use it to achieve excellence in all parts of your life. Set up a PRICE system for losing weight or running. Set one up for your kids' chores or school grades. If you involve your family you can make a New Year's resolution become a reality rather than another unfulfilled promise to yourself and others."

"It gives me another way to take what I know about One Minute Management and really put it to work in an organized fashion," said the veteran manager.

"It certainly has been key to our performance," said Smith.

"Have you ever had anyone resist paying the PRICE?" asked the veteran manager.

"Why don't you ask the One Minute Manager about Hank?" smiled Smith as she got up and led the veteran to the door.

"Yes, I guess I have taken enough of your time," said the veteran manager. "I've found this very practical and I appreciate your willingness to share your secrets with me."

"They're only secrets," responded Smith, "because people act as though they never knew them. Actually they're just common sense put to use."

As the veteran walked back to the One Minute Manager's office, he was amazed at how true that phrase was—common sense put to use.

When he got to the One Minute Manager's office, the veteran was greeted with a warm smile. "The PRICE is right, isn't it?" the One Minute Manager laughed.

"It sure is," said the veteran manager. "It really makes sense, but I have one question. Who is Hank?"

The One Minute Manager began to laugh. "I thought it was only a matter of time before someone told you about Hank. Why don't you sit down," said the One Minute Manager, "so I can tell you about him.

"When I first came here I heard about Hank from Steve Mulvany, a productivity-improvement consultant who had worked with our company. Steve said, 'Watch out for Hank when you start training the foremen about One Minute Management. He's one tough guy.' I got the impression that converting Hank to One Minute Management would be like persuading a charging rhino to rethink his strategy.

"The stories about Hank were widespread. He was almost a legend in his own time. For instance, I was told that one morning he got so mad at one of his people that he literally (I checked it out later with Hank and it was true) picked him up and hung him by his overalls on a nail and left him there until lunch."

"Now, how could anybody do that?" asked the veteran manager.

"Hank is about five feet nine by five feet nine and strong," said the One Minute Manager. "When he sits at the end of our thirty-inch-wide conference table he is about as wide as the table. He has arms as big as my thighs. His head sits on his shoulders as if he literally had no neck."

"He doesn't sound like a real attractive human being," said the veteran.

"No, he's not or at least he wasn't," said the One Minute Manager. "His eyes were bloodshot, he had an old grumpy voice, and he walked like a bear on the prowl.

"I first met Hank," continued the One Minute Manager, "at a training session. When I came here and began to implement One Minute Management, I initially did most of the training myself. I arrived early to the session where I met Hank. While I was setting up training materials in the front of the conference room, I suddenly got the feeling somebody was watching me. I turned around and there was Hank sitting alone at the other end of the conference room."

"How did you know it was him?" asked the veteran manager.

"I just knew," said the One Minute Manager. "Especially when I got no response to a smile. I could just feel his eyes looking through me."

"What did you say?" interrupted the veteran. "I feel as if I'm in the middle of another soap opera."

"Nothing then," said the One Minute Manager, "but I knew he was watching my every move. At least I sensed he was. When I started my session he sat quietly until I said, 'One of the keys to motivating your people is to catch them doing something right. When that occurs,' I asked, 'what should you do as a manager?' Everyone said reward or praise them, except Hank."

"How did you know he didn't agree?" said the veteran manager.

"Hank raised his hand," said the One Minute Manager, "and I thought to myself, 'Well, the session is over. Pack your bags.' He said, 'I want to say something,' and I said, 'Sure!'

"Hank said, 'I just want you to know that I use punishment and it works.'

"I looked at him and thought to myself, 'I'll bet it does.' What are you going to say to someone like Hank? He could have said that the sky was green and I would have agreed right there that the sky was green.

"When I got my composure, I said, 'That's interesting, Hank. Would you be willing to share the pros of punishment with the group?'

"He said, 'Sure! There are three: It's easy. It's fast. And it makes me feel good.'

"Looking at his size, I said to myself, 'I'll bet it works for you.' Then I said, 'If those are the pros, Hank, are there any cons to using too much punishment?'

"Hank smiled and said, 'I can't think of one.'

"I said, 'I can think of three areas too much punishment can affect—efficiency rates, absenteeism, and turnover.'

"Hank stared at me because he knew what I was thinking. He had the lowest efficiency rates in the plant. Now he knew that but I had heard his excuses: 'I have the toughest department' and 'I'm on a swing shift and everyone knows that swing shifts traditionally have the lowest productivity.'

"Absenteeism—Hank consistently had twenty percent of his people absent so he had eight out of ten at work most days. The personnel folks joked that without Hank's department they would have to lay off one staff member. They were busy every day processing transfer requests, terminations, or hiring for his department.

"Turnover—his was the highest in the plant. But I had heard him say, 'I manage the worst department there is and everyone likes to transfer out.'

"When it was obvious I was baiting him, Hank said, 'OK, boss. What do you expect me to do differently with bums like I've got? They live to pay for their booze. And besides, I don't like them and they don't like me.'

"I said, 'Hank, I know you probably think these sessions are a waste of time. But will you give me a chance?'

"'OK!' Hank said. 'But I'm not counting on anything.'

"After I had talked about the need to start any performance-improvement program with pinpointing the problem and then recording present performance, I shared the importance of the daily printout from the computer for tracking progress and giving people feedback. You see, in our operation the foremen get good information on performance."

"As you were speaking, what was Hank doing?" asked the veteran manager.

"He just sat there with his arms crossed," said the One Minute Manager. "There was no expression on his face."

"After the meeting, much to my surprise, Hank came up to me and said, 'Look, I think this stuff is probably useless. But I'd like to increase my efficiency rate. Any smart ideas?'

"'Every day you get a printout from the computer on the efficiency of each of your machines for the day before,' I replied. 'Since you have a one man per machine operation, this information tells you how each of your guys is doing. All I want you to do is make a graph for everyone and at the beginning of every morning, fill in the efficiency ratings on the graphs and then walk around and show each guy what his efficiency was from the day before. That's all I want you to do.'

"'OK,' said Hank. 'I'll give it a try even though I don't think it will work.'

"The next morning, I went down to see what happened," continued the One Minute Manager. "Hank got the printout from the computer and transferred the information to graphs for each of his people and then walked over to his first guy and said, 'Listen, don't give me any crap about the number on here. Just look at it.' And then he showed the guy his efficiency rating.

"I thought to myself, 'This is going to be a disaster,' so I said to Hank, 'Just show them the number and don't say anything else. Just say, "You got eighty-six percent efficiency yesterday." "You got ninety-four." "You got seventy-five."'

"When he said to the next guy, 'You got eighty-three percent efficiency yesterday,' the guy said, 'Hank, get out of here and get away from me. We're going to call the union. Knock this stuff off. Leave us alone. You've left us alone for years unless we did something wrong, so just get out of here.'

"Hank said to me, 'I told you they don't like me.'

"I said, 'Hank, keep trying.'

"Hank kept showing his guys their efficiency rates even though they were giving him a hard time and not even looking at their graphs. Then after about four days I could see them starting to look when he came along showing them their scores. They were starting to look at the graphs because they were beginning to get feedback and were able to compare how they did yesterday to the day before, and the day before that."

"And the comparisons were against themselves, not the other guys," interrupted the veteran.

"Yes," said the One Minute Manager. "We find it more constructive to have people competing against themselves and a performance standard rather than competing with each other."

"What happened next?" interrupted the veteran manager, anxious to get back to hearing about Hank.

"Hank told his people, 'Listen, you guys, I'm getting sick and tired of giving this feedback to you all. From now on, anybody with eighty-five percent or higher efficiency, I'll come and show you your rating. But if you didn't get eighty-five percent, you don't deserve to talk to me.'"

"Let's see if I can fit this story into the PRICE system," suggested the veteran. "When Hank said he wanted to improve efficiency he was pinpointing the problem. That's 'P.' When he made the graphs from the computer printout he was into 'R' for record. And when he began showing his folks their efficiency ratings in the beginning he was involving them, even if he was a little autocratic. That's 'I.' Now by deciding to talk only with people with eighty-five percent or higher efficiency, it sounds as if Hank was beginning to manage consequences and to coach. That's 'C.' That decision was made at his own kind of evaluation session: 'E.'"

"Exactly!" said the One Minute Manager. "You really learned the PRICE system quickly!"

"I just love the simplicity of it all," said the veteran manager.

"It was funny to see Hank," continued the One Minute Manager, "walk up to a guy and then, reading that his efficiency rate was below eighty-five, walk right by him without showing him his graph or saying a word. The expression on that person's face was priceless. He acted as if Hank had stabbed him in the back."

"I bet pretty soon everyone was getting over eighty-five percent efficiency," said the veteran manager.

"You better believe it," said the One Minute Manager. "After a week or so Hank called them all back together. He said, 'Ninety-five percent efficiency or I don't come to your machine.' It was amazing how their efficiency scores climbed."

"That's amazing, considering that all Hank was doing was giving them the information," said the veteran.

"Right," said the One Minute Manager. "He didn't say they did well; he didn't say they did badly. Just the fact that Hank would show up at their machines was important to them.

"He did this," continued the One Minute Manager, "for some time. Then, after about a month he gave each of them his own graph and stopped coming to their machines but he would leave the printout from the computer on his desk. I swear to you, nine out of ten guys would run over there on their break time to see what they got and go back and fill in their graphs.

"Then he started to circle in red the guys who got ninety-five percent. Can you believe it? A bunch of hard-nosed guys like this talking about whether they got a red circle that day. They thought it was really something special if they got a red circle."

"What was happening to the performance in Hank's department all this time?" asked the veteran manager.

"It was going up like a spaceship on the graph," said the One Minute Manager. "At the same time his absenteeism and tardiness were going down too. The other foremen didn't believe it. They thought Hank was cheating on the data. I knew he wasn't because I was watching the data all the time."

"What did he do next?" asked the veteran manager.

"One day," said the One Minute Manager, "he brought all his guys together and said, 'You guys have really been increasing your efficiency. I'll tell you what I'll do. My wife makes the finest pumpkin bread you've ever tasted, so if every guy in this department gets one hundred percent, I'll have her bring in pumpkin bread at lunchtime tomorrow for everyone '

"I wasn't at the meeting but I heard about it from the grapevine. I went to see him. I said, 'Hank, pumpkin bread as a motivator? It's not going to work.'

"He said, 'That's what you think. Let me do it.'

"I said, 'Hank, you can do anything you want'— as if I could stop him."

"Hank didn't even walk around and watch them," continued the One Minute Manager. "They monitored themselves. For example, if someone left his machine to get something or do something, one of the guys would yell, 'Hey, where are you going? You get back to work.'"

"Did everyone get one hundred percent efficiency?" asked the veteran manager.

"You better believe it," said the One Minute Manager. "No exceptions. So at lunchtime the next day Hank's wife brought in these platters of pumpkin bread. You never saw anything go so fast in your life. They loved it.

"I thought that was something, so I tried to replicate what Hank did for all of the departments.

"I called in my key people and told them I would be willing to buy lunch the next day for every department that got one hundred percent in efficiency on any given day."

"What did your people think?" asked the veteran.

"Everyone thought it was a great idea," said the One Minute Manager. "We had these little coupons printed up that the employees could use on the 'roach coach.'"

"The roach coach?" wondered the veteran.

"That's an affectionate name for the food truck that goes around to plants, selling all kinds of goodies," said the One Minute Manager. "Our folks often wait to eat lunch until it stops here.

"While I thought my plan was a good idea, it went over like a lead balloon. In fact, people got hostile. They were saying things like: 'This is ridiculous!' 'Don't have us do five hundred dollars more productivity in exchange for a two dollar food coupon. We're insulted.'"

"What happened?" asked the veteran manager.

"I was confused," said the One Minute Manager, "so I asked Hank to come see me."

"So Hank's now a consultant to top management," laughed the veteran.

"It took courage to admit I needed advice from Hank," confessed the One Minute Manager.

"What did Hank think of the program?" wondered the veteran manager.

"He had elected not to do the coupon program," said the One Minute Manager. "In fact, he was one of the leaders of the revolt. That's why I wanted to talk to him—to find out why he wouldn't participate in the coupon program.

"When Hank arrived at my office, I asked him, 'Why aren't you involved in the coupon program?'

"Hank leaned over to me and put his finger right in my face and said, 'You tried to bribe the employees. You offered them two dollars on the roach coach to increase productivity. Let me tell you how I and the other men felt about that. We were damn mad. We felt used and insulted.'

"Then he took his finger away from my face, paused, and stared in my eyes for what seemed like an endless moment. 'Let me tell you one other thing,' Hank said as he broke the silence. 'You're good. You've done a tremendous job putting the One Minute Manager to work here. We think you're better than that kind of bribery stuff.'

"Then Hank smiled and said, 'How's that for a One Minute Reprimand?'

"I'll have to admit that being on the end of a reprimand from Hank wasn't the most comfortable experience I've ever had," said the One Minute Manager.

"After I got my composure back, I said, 'I realize my mistake, but how was what I did different from your pumpkin bread?'

"'My wife made that pumpkin bread,' said Hank. 'I put myself out and so did she. You offered to give us two dollars to use on the roach coach. That's an insult and a bribe.'

"'So my lunch coupon,' I said, 'was insulting because it wasn't personal and it didn't involve any emotional commitment from me?'

"'Right,' said Hank. 'You have done a fantastic job around here introducing your concepts of One Minute Management and teaching us the ABC's. Most of us are willing to pay the PRICE to get good performance. The people you have working for you are winners and you shouldn't take the ball away from them. Don't try to sprinkle motivation from on high.'

"'I understand what you are saying, Hank,' I replied, 'and I appreciate your honesty.'

"That's OK,' said Hank. 'I've learned a lot here and there's no reason why I can't help you learn, too.'

"We both smiled and shook hands."

"Hank's quite a guy, isn't he?"* said the veteran manager.

"He certainly is," said the One Minute Manager. "It's people like him who have really made our efforts worthwhile here."

"And he's taught me to put the things I've learned here into a human perspective," added the veteran. "Speaking of the things I've learned, I'd like to sum it all up for you. I want to be certain I've got it all straight."

"Go right ahead," said the One Minute Manager.

---

*The Hank story is based on a real character. He models characteristics of many of the outstanding supervisors we have worked with over the years. Steve Mulvany, president of Management Tools, Inc., in Orange, California, originally developed the story while Bob Lorber was president and Steve was senior vice-president of PSI, a productivity-improvement company that conducted a project in Hank's plant. Steve supervised this project and since then has immortalized Hank as "Sid" in his seminars and presentations around the world.

"**F**IRST, I cleared up some questions I had about the three secrets of One Minute Management: One Minute Goal Setting, One Minute Praisings, and One Minute Reprimands," remembered the veteran manager. "Second, I've learned that the ABC's of Management (the Activators, the resulting Behavior, and the appropriate Consequences) help sequence those secrets in a way that makes them usable. And third, the PRICE System gives me a good handle on how to put the One Minute Manager to work in a systematic way that can be shared with everyone. It turns the secrets into skills and moves the application of One Minute Management beyond individuals to work groups and the organization as a whole."

The One Minute Manager smiled as he listened to the veteran. He loved to see the excitement that learning new things sparked in people.

"Sounds as if you have everything pretty straight," commented the One Minute Manager.

"I think I've got it," said the veteran. "I can't thank you enough for sharing with me what you know and have learned about management."

"It's my pleasure," said the One Minute Manager. "All that knowledge is to be shared. Let me leave you with one last thought. The best way to learn to be a One Minute Manager and to use what you have learned is to start to do it. The important thing is not that you do it right, but that you get under way. We have a saying here:

*

*Anything
Worth Doing
Does Not
Have To Be Done
Perfectly—
At First*

*

"THAT'S so true," said the veteran. "I'm really committed to getting started."

"It's not your commitment that I'm worried about," said the One Minute Manager. "It's your commitment to your commitment. For example, people say diets don't work. Diets work just fine—it's people who don't work. They break their commitment to their commitment to lose weight. I don't want you to do that with putting the One Minute Manager to work."

"What you're saying makes sense of what a friend of mine told me," said the veteran. "He told me I should give up trying. I should either do it or not do it."

"That's just what I was getting at," said the One Minute Manager. "To illustrate it, would you try to pick up that pen on the desk?"

The veteran went over to the desk and picked up the pen.

"I told you to try to pick up the pen. I didn't tell you to pick it up," said the One Minute Manager.

The veteran smiled.

"You got it," said the One Minute Manager. "You're either going to do it or not going to do it. Saying 'I'll try' just sets up all your past patterns which will result in your not doing it."

"Thanks for that final advice," said the veteran. "I certainly don't want to be the guy hanging on to the branch on the side of the mountain, yelling, 'Is there anybody else up there?'"

With that said, the veteran got up and put his hand out to the One Minute Manager. "I'm going to do it," he said with sincerity.

WHEN the veteran manager left the One Minute Manager's office, he was excited about implementing what he had learned. He was committed to his commitment.

The next day he began to do just that. He did not wait until he could do everything he had learned exactly right. He knew if he waited he would never get started, so he shared what he had learned with all his people, and they in turn shared it with their people. Everyone supported each other's efforts to put One Minute Management to work.

As he worked with his people, the veteran manager learned that four systems needed to be set up in the organization to make One Minute Management pay off. Employees needed to know: what they were being asked to do (accountability system); what good behavior looked like (performance-data system); how well they were doing (feedback system); and what they would get for good performance (recognition system).

Pretty soon, everyone in the veteran's organization set up PRICE projects for each One Minute Goal. The goals themselves identified the *pinpointed* areas of interest. Present performance on each of these goals was *recorded*. Then each employee was *involved* in goal setting, as well as in establishing coaching and counseling strategies. Then *coaching* began. Managers were responsive to their people's needs for supervision. Everybody wanted the others to win. When *evaluation* came around, progress was reviewed and new goals set.

Pretty soon the inevitable happened:

THE VETERAN MANAGER WAS SUCCESSFUL IN
PUTTING THE ONE MINUTE MANAGER TO WORK
AND IT MADE A DIFFERENCE —

People not only felt better, they performed
better. And more important, putting the One
Minute Manager to work made a difference where
it really counted—on the bottom line. Production
increased, quality improved, sales skyrocketed,
and retention and attendance of employees
surpassed all the companies in the area.

Everywhere the veteran manager went he
shared what he had learned with others. One
Minute Management soon became known as
Theory W. The One Minute Manager said, "You
can have your Theory X, Theory Y, and Theory Z.
We call One Minute Management **Theory W**
because it works."

Wherever the veteran manager went, he always
told people who had learned how to put the One
Minute Manager to work . . .

*

*Keep Your
Commitment
To
Your Commitment*

*And
Share
It
With
Others*

*

01 *Concept Praisings*

We would like to give a public praising to the following people whose conceptual contributions were invaluable to us in preparing this book:

David Berlo for his thoughtful analysis of why organizations are not good places for people to be.

Tom Connellan, *Aubrey Daniels*, and *Larry Miller* for teaching us many things about productivity improvement.

Werner Erhard for what he taught us about making life work and keeping your commitments.

Paul Hersey for his creativity and ability to integrate applied behavioral science theory.

Spencer Johnson for attaching the One Minute concept to praisings and reprimands.

Fred Luthans and *Robert Kreitner* for one of the first conceptualizations of the ABC's.

David McClelland for his pioneer work on achievement motivation.

Gerald Nelson for developing the One Minute Scolding, the forerunner of the One Minute Reprimand.

George Odiorne for his work on goal setting (MBO) and the "activity trap."

B. F. Skinner for his classic work on reinforcement theory.

Rick Tate for coining the phrase "Feedback Is the Breakfast of Champions."

01 Personal Praisings

We would like to give a public praising to a number of the important people in our lives who have influenced and supported us.

Ken Blanchard would like to praise:

Spencer Johnson, my co-author of *The One Minute Manager*, for being my writing partner, publishing mentor, and friend.

Kelsey Tyson for his creative marketing of the original version of *The One Minute Manager* and for his untiring dedication and devoted friendship.

Margaret McBride for being my literary agent, friend and mediator, and constant support.

All the folks at William Morrow and Company, Inc., particularly *Pat Golbitz* and *Larry Hughes*, for believing in Spencer and me and *The One Minute Manager*, and *Al Marchioni* and his people for distributing and selling the book.

The following top managers who believed in me and *The One Minute Manager* and gave us the kind of support that helped make the dream of a best-selling book a reality:

Roy Anderson	Dave Hanna	Bud Robinson
Rhett Butler	David Jones	Mike Rose
Jim DeLapa	Lou Neeb	Don Smith
Bob Davis	Ernie Renaud	Jere Thompson

Michael and *Nina Shandler*, two very talented writers and trainers, who literally lived with the manuscript during the middle drafts, and working with me, helped this book begin to change from a good book to what I think is a "super" book.

Ken Haff, *Laurie Hawkins*, *Drea Zigarmi*, and *Pat Zigarmi*, my colleagues and friends, for their ever-present love, support, and helpful feedback.

Paul Hersey for being my mentor, friend, father and brother—all wrapped up in one.

Eleanor Terndrup for being my talented secretary and second mother. From start to finish of this manuscript Eleanor was always there way beyond the call of duty.

Bernadette McDonald for her unfailing devotion and commitment to quality work. Without her typing and clerical skills during the middle drafts, this book would never have become a reality.

Lynette Grage for worrying about where we were going to get the money to pay for all my dreams.

Regina Rule, *Pat Nekervis*, and *Donna Hagen* for their constant hard work and caring about *The One Minute Manager*.

A special thanks to my mother and father, *Dorothy and Ted Blanchard*. Mom has been a constant inspiration and joy all my life but especially since Dad's passing. While he has not been here to share this One Minute Manager phenomenon with me, I have felt his support.

Bob Lorber would like to praise:

Gordon Anderson for giving me the opportunity to form my new Productivity Implementation Company and for teaching me that the United States is only one part of the world.

Linda Belton for her loyalty and extraordinary competence as my assistant during many of the productivity-implementation years.

Gene Bryan for making the computer come alive and computer-aided management a reality. And for being my co-author in our new book *The Profit Gap.*

Fred Chaney for being a mentor and for giving me the opportunity to found and build Performance Systems Improvement (PSI).

Bob Elliott for taking a risk, believing in me, and letting me personally implement our first productivity-improvement program.

Ethan Jackson for his exceptional business and personal advice and unconditional friendship. For modeling the critical balance of family and business and opening my eyes to the spiritual side of life.

Kef Kamai for being my partner, friend, and compadre and for making me pay attention to my health and physical fitness. For being Tracie's godfather and always being there when I need him.

Larry Miller for being an invaluable colleague and friend. And for being my East Coast partner in our productivity-improvement business.

Jim Morrell for his guidance, friendship, and influence on my career path.

Bud Ogden for opening the world of the coal industry and all its beauty, hardships, and real people, and for the major opportunities he personally provided.

Mark Rosen for being my first colleague in productivity implementation and for the many years of being a brother and friend.

Carl Samuels for his unselfish love, advice, and openness.

Donna Sillman for helping Ken and me edit the first draft of our book, and for staying in California to support the formation of our new company.

Fran Tarkenton for his energy, inspiration, and contributions to the field of productivity improvement.

Ed Winguth for always believing in me and in his continued help on complex career decisions.

A special thank you to my mother and father, *Rose and Jules Lorber*. They always understand me, support me, express their love, and practice the principles we have written about in our book.

About the Authors

Dr. Kenneth H. Blanchard, co-developer of the One Minute Manager and Situational Leadership, is an internationally known author, educator, and consultant/trainer, and professor of leadership and organizational behavior at the University of Massachusetts, Amherst. He has written extensively in the field of leadership, motivation, and managing change, including the widely used and acclaimed Prentice-Hall text *Management of Organizational Behavior: Utilizing Human Resources,* co-authored with Paul Hersey and now in its fourth edition, and the national best seller *The One Minute Manager,* William Morrow and Company, co-authored with Spencer Johnson, M.D.

Dr. Blanchard received his B.A. in government and philosophy from Cornell University, an M.A. in sociology and counseling from Colgate University, and a Ph.D. in administration and management from Cornell University.

As chairman of the board of Blanchard Training and Development, Inc., a San Diego-based human-resource-development company, Dr. Blanchard has trained over one hundred thousand managers and has advised a wide range of corporations and agencies. His approaches to management have been incorporated into many *Fortune* 500 companies as well as numerous fast-growing entrepreneurial companies.

Dr. Robert L. Lorber, an internationally known and recognized expert in performance improvement, is president of RL Lorber and Associates, Inc., a company specializing in the strategic design and implementation of productivity-improvement systems, headquartered in Orange, California.

Dr. Lorber received his B.A. and M.A. degrees from the University of California at Davis and a Ph.D. in Applied Behavioral Science and Organizational Psychology. His numerous publications include "Effective Feedback: The Key to Engineering Performance," "Managing Data vs. Gut Feeling," "How to Implement Change: Supervise and Lead," and "Productivity—in Five Intensive Lessons."

Dr. Lorber has spoken at many Young Presidents' Organization universities and area conferences. He is on the board of the Business School at the University of Santa Clara, the Board of Editors of the *Journal of Organizational Behavior Management,* and is a member of The Presidents Association of the American Management Association, the American Productivity Management Association, the American Psychological Association, and the World Affairs Council.

Dr. Lorber and his organization have implemented productivity systems for small, medium, and numerous *Fortune* 500 companies throughout the United States, as well as the Middle East, South America, Mexico, Africa, Europe, and Canada.

Services Available

Ken Blanchard and Robert Lorber work closely together and their two companies—Blanchard Training and Development, Inc., and RL Lorber and Associates, Inc.—have joined forces to help organizations both improve performance and increase human satisfaction.

Services available include: seminars ranging from two to five days; learning materials, from self-assessment instruments to audio and video programs; and ongoing consultation, from team building to long-term productivity implementation.

Putting the One Minute Manager to Work is also available: on videotape from CBS Fox Video, on audiotape from Nightingale-Conant Corporation, on computer software from Resource 1, Inc., in live-seminar format from Blanchard Training and Development, Inc., and RL Lorber and Associates, and at conventions and major meetings from Conference Speakers International.

For further information contact either:

Blanchard Training and Development, Inc.
2048 Aldergrove Avenue, Suite B
Escondido, California 92025 619/489-5005
or
RL Lorber and Associates, Inc.
505 South Main Street, Suite 1017
Orange, California 92668 714/541-5001

THE CASE OF THE
MISSING
DINOSAUR
EGG

The First Kids Mysteries

The Case of the Rock 'n' Roll Dog
The Case of the Diamond Dog Collar
The Case of the Ruby Slippers
The Case of the Piggy Bank Thief
The Case of the Missing Dinosaur Egg

THE CASE OF THE
MISSING
DINOSAUR
EGG

MARTHA FREEMAN

Holiday House / New York

Library of Congress Cataloging-in-Publication Data

Freeman, Martha, 1956-
The case of the missing dinosaur egg / by Martha Freeman.—1st ed.
p. cm. — (First kids mystery ; #5)
Summary: Seven-year-old Tessa and ten-year-old Cammie, daughters of the first female
president, and their dog Hooligan, investigate when an ostrich egg is substituted for
a rare dinosaur egg on loan from another country.
ISBN 978-0-8234-2523-5
1. White House (Washington, D.C.)—Juvenile fiction. [1. White House (Washington,
D.C.)—Fiction. 2. Presidents—Family—Fiction. 3. Sisters—Fiction. 4. Dogs—
Fiction. 5. Lost and found possessions—Fiction. 6. Washington (D.C.)—Fiction.
7. Mystery and detective stories.] I. Title.
PZ7.F87496Cap 2013
[Fic]—dc23

2012033735
ISBN 978-0-8234-3061-1 (paperback)

*For Professor Ann Marie Major,
in gratitude for her friendship,
her expertise and her students.*

CHARACTERS

Cameron Parks (Cammie), our narrator, is the
ten-year-old daughter of U.S. president Marilee Parks
and her husband, Rick. Since Cameron's mom was
inaugurated in January, she has lived in the White House
with her extended family.

Tessa Parks, Cameron's sister, is seven years old and a
drama queen.

Nathan Leone (Nate) is Cameron and Tessa's
cousin, the only child of their aunt Jen. Nate was born
in Korea. Aunt Jen adopted him as an infant and brought
him to live with her in San Diego. Now he and Aunt
Jen live with Tessa and Cameron's family in the White
House.

Jennifer Maclaren Leone (Aunt Jen) is Cameron
and Tessa's aunt and Nate's mom. A widow, she lives
with Nate in an apartment on the third floor of the

White House and acts as First Lady in President Parks's administration. President Parks is her younger sister.

Jeremy, Charlotte and Malik are Secret Service agents who help keep the First Family safe.

Mr. Morgan and Mr. Webb are security officers with the Smithsonian Institution. Previously, they helped Tessa, Cameron and Nate solve the Case of the Ruby Slippers.

Barbara Maclaren (Granny, aka Judge Maclaren) is Cameron, Tessa and Nate's grandmother. She used to be a judge in California, and before that a district attorney, and before that a police officer. When Cameron and Tessa's mom won the presidential election, Granny agreed to come to Washington to help take care of Cameron, Tessa and Nate.

Willis Bryant is Granny's special friend. He used to run the White House elevator but now works for Cameron's family, taking care of their too-energetic dog, Hooligan, on weekdays.

Jan and Larry (she's blond, he's not) are popular local newscasters in Greater Metropolitan Washington.

Marilee Maclaren Parks (Mom) is Cameron and Tessa's mom and, since January, the president of the United States. She's a lawyer, and she used to be a senator from California.

✖

Rick Parks (Dad) is Cameron and Tessa's dad. He has a job building airplanes in California, so he is usually in Washington only on weekends. He used to be an air force pilot.

Mr. Brackbill is the librarian at Cameron, Tessa and Nate's school.

Evgenia is in Cameron and Nate's fifth-grade class. She is very smart and quiet.

Hooligan is Cameron and Tessa's dog. He looks like a Dr. Seuss version of an Afghan hound. "Hooligan" is a word that means rowdy, but Hooligan is not really bad. He just has too much energy.

Ms. Ann Major is a deputy assistant press secretary in the office of President Parks. Her beagle, Pickles, has playdates with First Dog Hooligan.

Antonia Alfredo-Chin (Toni) is a friend of Cameron, Tessa and Nate's who also happens to be the niece of the president of a certain nearby nation and the daughter of its ambassador to the United States. She lives in Washington, D.C. Her dog, Ozzabelle, was a gift from Tessa and Cameron.

CHAPTER ONE

My little sister, Tessa, leaned over and whispered in my ear, "That is the biggest egg I ever saw."

True, it was a really big egg. But we were in the audience at a talk at a museum, and we were supposed to be quiet. I shushed my sister, but she ignored me.

"It makes sense, though, doesn't it, Cammie?" Tessa said. "Dinosaurs were big. So their babies were big. A big baby needs a big egg."

Now my cousin Nate joined in. "They're called hatchlings, not babies, Tessa." Nate is ten like me. Tessa is seven.

Nate's mom looked over at us, put her finger to her lips and nodded at the man who was talking. On the table in front of him was the gleaming, cream-colored egg.

I pointed at myself and shrugged, meaning *Me? I didn't do anything!*, which made Nate's mom—my aunt Jen—frown.

Oh, fine.

It was a Saturday afternoon in April, the week before Easter. Outside, it was a beautiful day. We live in Washington, D.C., and down by the Tidal Basin the cherry trees were blossoming. What I really wanted to do was go play outside with my dog, but instead I was cooped up with a bunch of ancient bones and grown-ups at the National Museum of Natural History.

Don't get me wrong. I like the museum, and I like dinosaurs. But when you're the kid of the president of the United States, like I am, you spend a little too much time being quiet and polite.

With no choice, I shook the wiggles out of my shoulders, resettled my posterior into the chair and tried to listen. The speaker's name was Professor Cordell Bohn, and he was a paleontologist—pronounced "pay-lee-un-TALL-uh-jist" —which is a person who studies long-ago plants and animals, like dinosaurs.

"Most people are surprised to learn that fossilized dinosaur eggs are reasonably common in many locations around the world," Professor Bohn was saying. "What's unique in this case, uh...unique—"

Professor Bohn stopped, looked down at the egg and raised his eyebrows. Was he listening to something?

A few seconds passed, nothing happened and Professor Bohn tried again.

"As I was saying, this find may help us better understand the link between dinosaurs and modern-day birds. We are hoping to study the shell—"

He stopped again, and this time everybody heard it—*rata-tap-tap-tap* coming from the egg.

What the heck?

Somebody gasped; other people whispered and pointed. Professor Bohn himself took a step backward but at the same time said, "There is no cause for alarm."

Meanwhile, my little sister leaned over. "Cammie? Is it going to hatch?"

Nate answered before I could. "Don't be ridiculous. Dinosaurs have been extinct for sixty-five million years."

Extinct or not, the *rata-tap* continued, and now the egg began to wobble!

To the left of me, a man wearing an untucked white shirt and black dress pants jumped up, ready to run. Next thing, the people beside him did the same; then...*rata-tata-tap*...*rata-tata-TAP*...*rata-tata-CRACK!* The eggshell broke and—right before our eyes—something damp, gray and funny-looking started to bust out!

CHAPTER TWO

"Gangway!" someone shouted, and a lot of people headed for the exits.

Meanwhile, a lady from the museum cried, "Ladies and gentlemen! Please exit in an orderly manner!"

Exit? Who wanted to exit? I wanted to see what was in that egg! But then my little sister sprang up, and of course I had to comfort her. "Don't worry, Tessa. It's much too small to hurt us."

"I know that—*duh*. I just want a closer look!" And— before Aunt Jen or the Secret Service could stop her— Tessa started climbing over chairs to get to the front of the room.

Aunt Jen sputtered, "Oh, for Pete's sake!" and climbed after Tessa, except Aunt Jen was wearing a narrow skirt and high heels, so navigating chairs was maybe not her most graceful maneuver. Nate and I tried not to laugh as she tripped and stumbled forward, but in the confusion, I was pretty sure no one else even noticed.

Meanwhile, I wished I could see what the egg was doing, but there were too many bodies in front of me.

"Jeremy!" I looked around for the tallest Secret Service agent. "Can you see?"

Jeremy stood on tiptoes. "Looks like the little fella's making progress," he said. "There's part of its head and maybe a shoulder...er, if it's even got shoulders."

"Does it have a crest—can you see?" Nate wanted to know. "Like a velociraptor?"

"What about huge, deadly teeth?" I asked. "Like T. rex?"

Jeremy shook his head. "Hard to tell from here. But if I had to guess, I'd say it had a beak and damp little feathers."

Nate nodded. "That makes sense. The latest research indicates many dinosaurs did have feathers."

I said, "Wait—I thought according to you it couldn't be a dinosaur."

My cousin shrugged. "It's a dinosaur egg, isn't it?"

Over all the noise in the room, I heard something new—laughter, which turned out to be Professor Bohn's.

"Ladies and gentlemen," he said, "if I can reclaim your attention? I'm afraid those of you hoping for something prehistoric are going to be disappointed. On the other hand, you could call this chick a modern-day dinosaur."

Nate grabbed my arm. "Come on. Let's get closer to the action."

Jeremy followed us as we made our way through the crowd. Soon we could see the chick's busy beak, chipping away at its prison, and pieces of white shell littering the floor and table.

"Hey," I said when I finally got a good look. "I've got a book about birds at home. Isn't that an ostrich?"

Professor Bohn heard me and nodded. "Very good, Cameron."

"I knew that," said Nate quickly.

Tessa shook her head. "Wow—nature is sure awesome! Who'd've thought an ostrich could come out of a dinosaur egg?"

Professor Bohn made a face that meant he was trying not to smile. "Well, actually, Tessa, the truth is this egg never belonged to a dinosaur. Dinosaur eggs, as you'll see when you tour the rest of the exhibit, are fossilized and look like rocks."

Aunt Jen said, "In that case, you must have known this egg belonged to a bird. Why didn't you say anything?"

Professor Bohn looked down at his shoes. "My bad." Then he looked up, and I noticed there were lots of laugh crinkles around his eyes. "I have a soft spot for pranks, and it was obvious to me that's what this was. I didn't want to spoil the fun, so I'm afraid I asked the museum staff if we could wait and see how it played out."

My aunt does not have what you'd call a big sense of humor. Without smiling, she nodded and said, "Ah."

Meanwhile, Nate asked, "Where's the real dinosaur egg?"

Professor Bohn started to answer, but the lady from

the museum beat him to it. "Nothing to worry about. We have the case well in hand."

"Case?" Tessa perked up. "Are you saying there's a mystery?"

"Oh, no, no, no." The lady shook her head. "It's not a mystery at all. The egg has, uh…just been misplaced. I'm sure it will turn up soon."

CHAPTER THREE

Tessa folded her arms across her chest and frowned. "Well, *that's* disappointing." The other grown-ups all looked super serious, but Professor Bohn laughed.

I was beginning to think I liked Professor Bohn.

Also, I knew what Tessa was thinking. She wanted a new mystery for us to solve! Since January, when Mom got to be president and our family moved into the White House, Nate, Tessa and I have investigated four different cases—and we've even been on the news.

By now we could see the ostrich chick's head—big beady eyes and a fierce-looking beak at the top of a long spotted neck. Honestly? It was ugly. But I remembered one time we had chicken eggs hatch in my class at school. The chicks started off disgusting, but then they dried off, fluffed up and got cute.

Tessa must have had the same idea, because she said, trying to sound casual about it, "So, who gets to keep the ostrich?"

"Oh, no." Aunt Jen shook her head. "Unh-unh, Tessa. Not happening."

Tessa said, *"Ple-e-ease,"* Aunt Jen said, *"No-o-o,"* and finally a guy in a blue shirt explained it would take the chick hours to get out of its egg, and then it would need to be washed in special soap to kill germs, and after that it would have to live in a special kind of electric box for a few days while it got used to life in the world.

"As it's growing up, it needs a pen and the company of other chicks," he said. "Plus there's one more thing. About half of ostrich chicks die...even if you do everything right."

My sister looked horrified.

Aunt Jen said, "You seem to know a lot about ostriches."

The man smiled and said he worked at the National Zoo. "We don't have ostriches," he said, "but we have rheas and emus, which are also ratites—big birds that don't fly."

Aunt Jen looked at Tessa. "Since the zoo has the equipment to raise a chick, why don't we let them take care of this guy? Then when he's bigger, you can go visit."

Tessa sighed. "I guess, but can we name him, at least?"

"What did you have in mind?" Aunt Jen asked.

"Uh..." Tessa looked at me. "Cammie, you do it."

I grinned. "Isn't it obvious? Dino!"

By this time, almost everyone had left the lecture room. Some of them were probably still running for their lives, but the rest were looking at the dinosaur egg exhibit, which was down a hallway. Professor Bohn said he didn't mind losing his audience. Nothing he had been planning to say was as exciting as watching a dinosaur egg hatch.

"Since we're finished here, would you kids like to take a quick tour of the exhibit?" Professor Bohn asked us.

We kids never had a chance to answer. Aunt Jen did it for us: "They would *love* to."

CHAPTER FOUR

Professor Bohn led us to the exhibit hall, where a sign over the doorway read: CRACKING UP: THE INNER LIVES OF DINOSAUR EGGS.

We went in. Along one wall there were windows looking onto 3-D scenes of mama dinosaurs taking care of eggs and hatchlings. In the middle of the room were glass cases containing real fossilized eggs and the fossils of young dinosaurs. A few contained fossils of broken eggs with the bones of never-hatched hatchlings inside.

Poor hatchlings.

The reason the fossils look like rocks, Professor Bohn explained, is simple: They *are* rocks. An egg fossil is made when an egg gets buried in sand and the sand gets flooded with water. Over millions of years, minerals in the water mix with minerals in the eggshell and form rock.

Here are some more things I learned about dinosaur eggs that day:

- Dinosaur nests have been found at more than two hundred sites around the world.
- In Montana, a whole lot have been found that were made by a kind of dinosaur that took really good care of its hatchlings.
- Most dinosaurs buried their eggs in leaves, grass or dirt to keep them warm and safe.
- The biggest dinosaur eggs are about two feet long, and the smallest are about the size of goose eggs.

It's true I started the afternoon with a bad attitude, but the stuff Professor Bohn told us was pretty cool—especially what he told us last.

"The more we learn about dinosaurs, the more we find out how much they're like birds," he said. "They apparently had feathers—"

"I knew that," Nate said.

"—and their eggs and bodily structure are also avian, which means birdlike. In fact, some scientists believe birds and dinosaurs are the same type of animals and shouldn't be considered separate at all."

By then it was time for us to leave the museum.

"What did you think of the exhibit, kids?" a reporter called as we walked through the rotunda. That's the big round room at the front where there's a huge stuffed African bull elephant.

Nate and I smiled, gave thumbs-up signs and kept walking.

But Tessa stopped, which—as usual—caused all the photographers in the room to go crazy snapping pictures. "We saw a dinosaur hatch," she said. "It was so-o-o cool!"

The reporter scribbled something, and a lot of people laughed. Aunt Jen said, "A dinosaur, Tessa? Or an ostrich?"

"Same thing!" Tessa said. "That's what Professor Bohn told us."

This led to more questions, and Tessa would happily have stayed all day, explaining and having her picture taken, but Aunt Jen thanked the news guys and shooed us forward. Meanwhile, Professor Bohn and the woman from the museum hung back and took questions. The woman was a paleontologist, too: Professor Teresa Rexington. She and Professor Bohn and a team of scientists from a certain nearby nation had found the dinosaur egg fossil that was now missing.

Our van was parked outside at the curb. We were about to climb in for the short ride home when I noticed two familiar men on their way up the steps to the museum. Among all those people wearing jeans and T-shirts, they stood out because they were wearing suits.

Nate had seen them, too, and he nudged me. "Cammie, isn't that—"

"Mr. Morgan and Mr. Webb!" I waved. "Hey, hi! How are you?"

Mr. Morgan and Mr. Webb are security guys for the Smithsonian. Now they came over to the van and nodded hello. Neither of them smiles much, and Mr. Webb hardly even talks.

Tessa got right to the point. "Are you here to investigate the missing egg? It's okay"—she winked—"you can tell us."

Mr. Morgan made sure no one was listening before he answered: "In fact, we may need to ask for your help. From what we've been told, the situation is, uh...complicated."

Tessa pumped her fist. "*Woot*—I knew it! The First Kids are back on the job!"

CHAPTER FIVE

Or were we?

All the rest of that day, we waited for a call...but none came.

I did get my wish to play with our big furry mutt, Hooligan, outside on the South Lawn. Nate practiced piano—did I mention he is some kind of piano genius? And Tessa cleaned up after the stray cat and kittens we found a couple of weeks ago near the Rose Garden. They live mostly in a box in Hooligan's room, which is two doors down from ours on the White House second floor.

Tessa and I ate dinner with Granny and her special friend, Mr. Bryant. Nate ate with his mom in their apartment on the third floor. After Mr. Bryant went home, Tessa, Nate and I played a few hands of hearts with Granny in the solarium, which is kind of like our rec room.

Finally, Granny announced it was time for bed, but

Tessa wanted to stay up and watch Jan and Larry, our favorite TV newscasters.

"Maybe the dinosaur exhibit will be on," Tessa said.

"You just want to see if *you're* on," Nate said.

Tessa didn't disagree, and Granny said, "Okay, five more minutes."

Nate grabbed the remote, turned on the TV and...

Uh-oh.

What we saw wasn't Tessa or a dinosaur egg; it was Aunt Jen's posterior as she hurdled and climbed over chair backs! At least the only visible underwear was her slip's lacy hem. Watching it, Nate was so embarrassed he had to close his eyes.

On TV, Larry tried to sound serious: "...First Auntie Jennifer Leone making a heroic attempt to catch First Daughter Tessa Parks at the National Museum of Natural History today...," while in the background Jan was giggling so hard she hiccupped.

After that, the view switched to some egg fossils, Nate and me doing the thumbs-up and Tessa saying we'd seen a dinosaur hatch.

Then Professor Bohn and the paleontologist from the museum, Professor Rexington, explained a little about birds and dinosaurs.

Finally, Jan said, "On a more serious note, Larry, unnamed sources tell us tonight that one of the dinosaur eggs from the exhibit has gone missing." The screen showed a picture of the missing egg, which sure enough, looked like a gray, egg-shaped rock. "And because the egg was a rare specimen excavated at a site in a certain nearby nation, its disappearance could have international political implications."

Larry cut in: "You mean this story is no yolk, Jan?"

Jan rolled her eyes. "You're hilarious, Larry."

After that they cut to a commercial, Granny said, "Bedtime," and Nate turned off the TV.

A ramp leads from the solarium down to the White House third floor. Walking down it, I asked Granny if she knew what Jan and Larry had meant about the missing egg having "international political implications."

Granny shrugged. "Try asking your parents," she said. "It's a mystery to me."

One thing about having your mom be president of the United States—you don't get to see her all the time. That Saturday evening, she and Dad had to go to some dinner thing. Tessa and I were in bed reading when they came in to say good night.

"Mama!" Tessa said. "I need a snuggle! Hi, Daddy! Explain about the dinosaur egg, please. Granny said you could."

Mom sat down on the edge of Tessa's bed, and Dad sat down on the edge of mine. The White House has tons of bedrooms, but we share because when we first moved in, neither one of us wanted to sleep alone.

"What dinosaur egg?" Dad asked. He was wearing a tuxedo, and Mom had on a dark-red dress and white beads.

Tessa told them how one was missing from the museum, and Mom said, "Oh, dear, muffin—it's complicated." She looked at Dad.

He closed his eyes, yawned and nodded all at the same time. "I guess there's a legend in this certain nearby nation that no life existed there in prehistoric times—not even dinosaurs. Supposedly, the first life didn't come until much later, when a heroic leader arrived and founded a city. After that came llamas and pyramids and cocoa beans and...well, you get the idea."

Tessa shook her head. "No, I don't."

But I thought I understood. "Jan and Larry said the egg was found in a certain nearby nation, right? So if that's true, the legend is wrong. There must've been dinosaurs there after all."

Tessa shrugged. "Oh, okay. But big whoop."

"Big whoop," Mom repeated, "unless you're the president of the certain nearby nation and you claim to be the great-great-and-so-on-grandson of the heroic leader. In fact, you claim that's one reason you're entitled to be president in perpetuity."

"What's per-pe-whatever you said?" Tessa wanted to know.

"Forever," Dad said. "In other words, instead of having elections and somebody new getting to be president, you just stay president."

Tessa looked horrified. "Oh, *no*! You don't want to do that, Mama, do you?"

Mom looked tired. "Not tonight, I don't."

"But wait a second," I said. "The president of the certain nearby nation is Manfred Alfredo-Chin, right? Whose dog is Hooligan's friend? Whose niece is our friend, Toni?"

Dad nodded. "That's the guy."

"So if everybody found out the legend's wrong because now there's this dinosaur egg, it might be bad for President Alfredo-Chin," I said. "And he's already got trouble because of those protests going on in his nation."

In case you hadn't guessed, my little sister is a drama queen. Now she waved her arms the way she does. "Oh, come on! No way did President Manfred Alfredo-Chin ever steal any dinosaur egg! First, he's our friend. Second, he doesn't even live here. And third, presidents don't do stuff like that—do they, Mama?"

Mom said, "I have never personally stolen a dinosaur egg, nor, to the best of my knowledge, has anyone on my staff."

Dad rolled his eyes. "Honey? You know you're speaking to your family, right? You're not on television."

Mom smiled. "Right. Anyway, I doubt President Alfredo-Chin is responsible for the missing egg. If I had to guess, I'd say the problem is at the museum. And now, muffins . . ." She stood up and yawned. "I am going to say good night. Church tomorrow, remember? It's Palm Sunday."

CHAPTER SIX

The next day started out normal...but got abnormal fast.

The normal part was Granny waking us for church at eight o'clock. But ten minutes later Charlotte knocked on Tessa's and my door while we were getting dressed. Charlotte is my favorite Secret Service agent.

"Mr. Webb and Mr. Morgan are in the Treaty Room, and they'd like to meet with you before church," she said. "Nate is on his way down."

Tessa didn't say a word—just yanked her dress over her shoulders and headed for the door.

"Shoes, Tessa?" I said. "Hair?"

"My hair's fine, and you can bring my shoes, okay? I'm in a hurry! But, oh..." She doubled back, opened her closet and grabbed a pink spangled baseball cap, the one she wears for detecting. "Don't forget your notebook!" she told me, and left.

Oh, Tessa.

I stepped into my own shoes, picked Tessa's up off the floor, got my notebook and a pen and followed.

When we first moved here, the house seemed huge—more like a hotel than a place to live. But now I'm getting used to it—paintings, chandeliers, antiques, elevators and just plain bigness everywhere.

The first floor, the State Floor, is basically a public place. Tourists come through most mornings, and there're always staff and marines around. Up here on the second and third floors, though, it's usually just the family and our guests and maybe housekeepers cleaning. Even so, it's big and fancy, and you never get away from the history.

Like now when I walked out our bedroom door? There was a window to my right at the end of the hall. It looks out over the North Portico—the front door—and it's where Abraham Lincoln stood to make his last speech.

The Treaty Room, where we were meeting Mr. Morgan and Mr. Webb, is across the Center Hall from our bedroom. Like a lot of presidents, my mom uses it as an office sometimes. There are some famous paintings in it, besides a big desk President Ulysses S. Grant used for cabinet meetings.

Now when I walked in carrying my notebook and Tessa's shoes, Mr. Webb and Mr. Morgan were sitting on a sofa holding coffee mugs, Tessa was sitting across from them in a chair and Granny and Charlotte were standing beside her. Nate wasn't there yet—no surprise. He is not a morning person.

I gave Tessa her shoes. "Granny said I can have coffee," she told me as she buckled them, "because this is a business meeting."

Coffee tastes terrible, but no way would I let my little sister out-grown-up me. "Can I, too?" I asked.

Granny said, "Yes you *may*," and rang for Mr. Patel, the cutest White House butler. Meanwhile, Nate came in, looking sleepy.

When we were settled, Mr. Morgan thanked us for agreeing to meet so early.

"No problemo!" said Tessa. Then she took a sip and made a face. "Is this what coffee's supposed to taste like?"

Granny got her some sugar.

Mr. Morgan continued, "Mr. Webb and I started our investigation into the missing egg at the museum yesterday. But we've run into some roadblocks, and we're hoping you can help."

"Actually, Mr. Morgan," Tessa interrupted, "we have already solved the case."

Mr. Morgan looked surprised, but not half as surprised as me, Nate and Granny. "What are you talking about?" I asked.

Tessa waved her arms the way she does. "What Mom and Dad said last night—*duh!* President Manfred Alfredo-Chin stole the dinosaur egg!"

This was not the first time Tessa had changed her mind overnight. But Nate, Granny and Charlotte hadn't been there when Mom and Dad told us about the legend, so I filled them in.

"Thank you, Cameron," Mr. Morgan said. "Mr. Webb and I are also aware of the issues in a certain nearby nation. However, our initial investigation indicates they are irrelevant."

"What's 'ir-rel-e—'?" Tessa started to ask.

"Doesn't matter," Nate said.

"It matters to *me!*" Tessa said.

"I mean the word 'irrelevant' means it doesn't matter," Nate said. "So Mr. Morgan's saying President Alfredo-Chin didn't steal the dinosaur egg."

"That is our opinion at this time," said Mr. Morgan.

"Well, *that's* a relief," said Tessa. "But then who did?"

Sometimes I can't believe my sister. "Tessa—if they knew that, they wouldn't be asking us to help, would they?"

Tessa was ready to admit I was right—except before she could, Mr. Morgan proved I was wrong. "We are confident we know who stole the egg," he said. "Professor Cordell Bohn."

CHAPTER SEVEN

If I were dramatic like my sister, I would have jumped out of my chair, waved my arms and probably stomped my feet.

I liked Professor Bohn! He knew interesting stuff about dinosaurs, and besides, he was smiley and funny and not like the other so-serious grown-ups. I didn't want him to be an egg thief, and I didn't believe he was one, either.

But I am not dramatic like my sister. So what I did instead was ask very, very calmly, "How do you know?"

Mr. Morgan explained.

It turned out he and Mr. Webb had spent Saturday afternoon and evening interviewing Professor Bohn, Professor Rexington and a few other people. What they learned was that Professor Rexington had been waiting for the dinosaur egg to arrive from a certain nearby nation all week. Then, at lunchtime Friday, a wooden crate showed up on her desk.

"It was the right kind of crate with the right kind of

label," Mr. Morgan said. "Naturally, she assumed it was the dinosaur egg."

"Wait a second," said Tessa. "What do you mean it 'showed up'? Didn't someone bring it to her?"

"Someone must have, but she was at lunch, and we don't know who," Mr. Morgan said.

"Write that down, Cammie," Tessa said.

I held up my notebook so Tessa could see I already had. Tessa nodded. "Good work. So then what happened?"

Mr. Morgan explained that inside the crate, Professor Rexington found the gleaming, cream-colored ostrich egg, wrapped in crumpled newspaper and brown straw.

"She knew right away it belonged to an ostrich," said Mr. Morgan, "and she immediately notified Professor Bohn. Rather than being upset, he was amused. He told her he fully expected the egg fossil to show up later in the day."

"But it didn't," Nate said.

Mr. Morgan nodded. "And when it didn't, he decided to use the ostrich egg as a prop for his talk and see what happened. Meanwhile, they reported the missing egg to security."

"So that's where you come in," Nate said.

Mr. Morgan nodded. "We tried to trace the real dinosaur egg's route to the United States. Apparently, it was shipped from the airport in the capital of a certain nearby nation. The shipping records show the crate was scanned into the system when it arrived at Dulles airport here in the United States. After that, the crate seems to have disappeared. We think the thief must have picked it up from the airport here, but we can't find any record of that."

For a moment the room was quiet except for the sound of me writing. When I had caught up with my notes, I realized something: "This is all pretty mysterious, but none of it says Professor Bohn is the thief."

Mr. Webb said, "On the contrary," and I almost dropped my pen because that was five whole syllables, and Mr. Webb never says anything!

Mr. Morgan nodded. "We were suspicious. Why did Professor Bohn insist the ostrich egg was only a harmless prank?"

"Uh...," I said, "because that's what he really thought?"

"Or," said Mr. Morgan, "because he wanted to delay a full investigation as long as possible. And there is something else. Late last night we made a call to Washington's top ten p.m. news team: Jan and Larry."

"Hey, wow—what a coincidence," said Tessa. "We watch Jan and Larry, too!"

Mr. Morgan nodded. "Everybody does. And when Mr. Webb and I heard the broadcast last night, we zeroed in on one thing: the identity of the 'unnamed sources' who told them about the egg's link to politics in a certain nearby nation."

"Jan and Larry don't have to name their sources," Nate said. "Freedom of the press is protected by the First Amendment to the Constitution."

"True," said Mr. Morgan. "But when national security is involved, the news media is often willing to cooperate. Also, I went to high school with Jan."

"So who told them?" Tessa asked.

Mr. Morgan raised his eyebrows: "Professor Cordell Bohn."

Tessa shook her head. "Uh-oh, Cammie. This is not looking good."

Meanwhile, Granny said, "Let me see if I've got this straight. You think Professor Bohn called Jan and Larry to suggest that the theft was connected to politics. You think he was trying to shift attention away from the truth—that he's the thief."

Mr. Morgan nodded. "Exactly right."

I had more questions, but Charlotte looked at her watch. "Ahem? It is getting a bit late if the children are going to get to church."

Mr. Morgan and Mr. Webb stood up to leave. "We have a plane to catch." They were on their way to Pittsburgh, Professor Bohn's hometown, to continue their investigation.

"What do you want us to do?" Tessa asked.

"While we're confident we have identified the thief," said Mr. Morgan, "we lack the proof we need. What we're hoping you can do is help us get that proof."

CHAPTER EIGHT

After fast good-byes, Granny hustled us into the Family
Kitchen, which is also on the White House second floor.
There, Tessa, Nate and I poured our coffee down the
sink and grabbed bagels with peanut butter to eat on
the way.

Downstairs, three cars were waiting for us. Granny
goes to one church, Aunt Jen and Nate go to another—
and my family goes to the Methodist one by Dupont
Circle. It's the same one we started going to eight years
ago when my mom got elected senator and we moved to
Washington from California.

I like going to church. Mom, Dad, Tessa and I get
to be together. We sing. The light coming through the
stained-glass windows makes pretty patterns on the
floor.

Because it was Palm Sunday, the service began with
the choir coming in waving palm branches and calling,
"Hosanna!" After that, we sang a hymn; then a lady

read Bible verses about how Jesus was the prophet of Nazareth.

Finally, the pastor stood up to speak. I tried to pay attention, but I had so much to think about! Solving a new mystery and finding an ancient dinosaur egg sounded fun. Gathering evidence to prove a nice man was a thief? Not so fun. But maybe Mr. Morgan and Mr. Webb were wrong. Maybe the evidence would show that somebody else stole the dinosaur egg.

I remembered what Mr. Morgan had said about the case and realized right away there was something that didn't make sense, something that might be a clue: the wooden crate with the ostrich egg that showed up on Professor Rexington's desk.

How did it get there, anyway?

I pictured a crate floating through the entrance of the museum and pushing buttons on the elevator...and I cracked myself up, which made Mom, Dad and Tessa all look over at me.

Oops.

Sorry, I mouthed.

Now the minister was talking about Jesus riding on a donkey, which made me picture a crate on the back of a donkey...and soon I was thinking about the case again.

By the time the minister said he would see us all next week to celebrate Easter Sunday, I had thought up the first step of a plan to solve the mystery, find the dinosaur egg and—by the way—prove to Mr. Morgan and Mr. Webb that even if Professor Bohn liked to joke around, he wasn't actually a bad guy.

All I needed was a single, solitary secret weapon—which luckily was not a problem. Right now, the one I had in mind was probably having a late-morning snooze.

It didn't take much convincing to get Nate and Tessa to go along with my plan; neither of them had a better idea. So that same afternoon, the three of us—along with Malik, one of the Secret Service agents, and our secret weapon—were in a White House van on our way back to the National Museum of Natural History. It closes at five on Sunday, so by five-thirty it was pretty empty.

The secret weapon was on a leash, because otherwise I was pretty positive he'd chew up some ancient, priceless bone or spider or piece of an asteroid.

Like you've probably figured out, the weapon I'm talking about is Hooligan, our big furry mutt. Hooligan looks like a cross between an Afghan hound and a Dr. Seuss character, which my dad says is because he's a mad mix-up of just about every kind of dog ever. Last time we went detecting, we found out Hooligan's nose must've come from a bloodhound, because he sure can track a scent.

But was last time just beginner's luck?

We were about to find out.

CHAPTER NINE

Professor Rexington met us inside the museum and led us through back hallways to a staff elevator that went up to the top floor, where her office is. Unlike Professor Bohn, Professor Rexington is not the most cheerful person ever. She hardly smiled when she said hello. But maybe she was just tired? There were circles under her eyes, same as my mom gets when she's stressed out.

Finally, we arrived at her office. The door was open, and we went in.

"You wanted to see the desk where the crate arrived, right? Well, this is it." Professor Rexington nodded at a big wooden desk with a neat stack of papers on top.

Meanwhile, our secret weapon wagged his tail and started sniffing inside a metal wastebasket beside the desk. It was full of crumpled newspaper and brown straw stuff.

"Oh, yeah," I said, "is that the packing material that was around the ostrich egg?"

Professor Rexington nodded. "Yes. I remember

thinking the straw looked like nesting material—appropriate for an egg."

"Can we see the crate, too?" Tessa asked.

Professor Rexington frowned. "I'm afraid I might've recycled it already–let me check."

She went through a door to another room and rustled around. While we waited, Hooligan continued to sniff.

"Good puppy! Smart puppy!" Tessa threw her arms around him. "You already know what you're supposed to do!"

My idea was for Hooligan to get the scent of the crate, then follow it backward from the desk. There are a ton of entrances to the museum. Knowing which one the crate came through might help us figure out how it got to the museum and who sent it.

Hooligan waited patiently for Tessa to be done hugging him; then he got back to work. At the same time, I knelt and looked at the date on the newspapers— Thursday, April 6, last Thursday. I pointed this out to Nate. He nodded and said since the crate arrived at the museum on Friday, it must have been packed and sent right away.

Meanwhile, Professor Rexington came back in with a slat of splintered wood and said, "Bad news. This is all that's left."

I examined the piece of wood, but there were no markings on it. Then I gave it to Hooligan to sniff. Did it smell like anything to him? Or were the different smells in the wastebasket confusing? For all I knew, somebody's lunch leftovers were in there.

My great idea didn't seem so great anymore. But it was too late to worry about that now. I would just have to trust our dog.

"Ready?" I said.

Malik, Tessa and Nate nodded.

"Okay." I took the leash and stood up. "Hooligan— go find!"

CHAPTER TEN

Note to self: next time you track anything with Hooligan, let Malik hold the leash.

Hooligan was so excited and took off so fast he nearly separated my arm from my shoulder, not to mention that no one could keep up with us.

"Hoo-Hoo-Hooligan! Slow down!" Tessa whined, but our dog didn't listen. Instead, nose held high, he galloped one way then the other down the corridors.

Was he really tracking a scent?

Or did he think we were playing tag?

Whatever it was, he was having a great time, and only skidded to a stop when he reached an impenetrable barrier—closed elevator doors.

This was a different elevator from the one we came up in. Nate, Tessa, Malik and Professor Rexington were way behind us by now, and before they could come near, Hooligan did one of the amazing tricks he's learned since coming to live in the White House: he jumped up and pushed the elevator call button with his paw.

The elevator car must've been waiting, because the doors opened instantly, and Hooligan looked around like, *We don't have to wait for those slowpokes, do we, Cammie?*

Well, of course we had to wait for them! I am not allowed to go anywhere without the Secret Service, in this case Malik—and he was bringing up the rear so he could keep Tessa and Nate in sight.

Thinking, *No problem, I know how to hold an elevator,* I let Hooligan tug me inside, but then, before I could stop him, he did it again—jumped up and pushed a button on the panel.

"Oh, no you don't!" I started looking frantically for the button that opens the doors, but there were a lot of floors in the building and a lot of buttons, too! By the time I finally found the right one, the doors were shut and the elevator had creaked into gear.

"Hooligan!" I said. *"Bad dog!"*

He didn't pay any attention, just sniffed the air, the walls and the corners. He was tracking something, but was it an ancient dinosaur egg? Or a stale turkey sandwich?

Down, down and down the elevator dropped into the museum's unknown depths. On the way, I had plenty of time to think…and to worry. When finally we came to rest, we were someplace called Level D.

D for Dungeon?

The second the doors cracked open, Hooligan shot

through, dragging me so fast my shoulders bumped one after the other—*Ouch! ouch!*—and before I even blinked, we were galloping top speed down what I think was a corridor, but I'm not sure because it was pitch-black and I couldn't see a thing!

CHAPTER ELEVEN

Can dogs see in the dark the way cats can? Why, oh, why, had I never looked this up?

I don't know how long we ran or where we went, but just when my legs were ready to quit, Hooligan put on a burst of speed, the leash slipped out of my hand and I flew headlong into something big and solid and...*furry*?

Still blind, I backed up and hit another hard, furry something, turned left and...*Ouch!*—something sharp! A claw? A tooth?—then right and...*bump, tumble, somersault*—I was suddenly sitting on the cold, hard floor and trapped for sure, with big, furry, sharp-clawed somethings closing in around me.

What did I do?

I screamed!

And then the lights came on. Now it was glare that blinded me, but I could still hear—the *click-click-clickety* of galloping doggy toenails, and then a man's voice: "What is going on in here?"

I blinked; my eyes focused, and here came my faithful dog on a mission to rescue me not only from this grumpy man but from a room full of life-size lions and tigers and bears—oh, my!

They were everywhere, each one stiff and staring just like the big African elephant in the rotunda upstairs.

Hooligan plowed into me a second later—*Oof!*—and licked my face—*Ewww!*—and for a few moments I just sat there breathing while the grumpy man sputtered about "unauthorized kids" and "trespassing" and "valuable exhibits."

Then he got a good look at me. "Y-y-you're Cameron Parks!"

I nodded. "Yes, I am. And I'm very sorry to be trespassing. And if you'll give me a second, I'll explain."

By the time Malik, Nate, Tessa and Professor Rexington arrived, Mr. Clark had introduced himself, and I had told him how Hooligan was tracking a wooden crate that used to contain an ostrich egg. Level D was not the dungeon. It was a subbasement storage area for old museum exhibits like these stuffed hunting trophies.

Hooligan wasn't done tracking yet, and now, trotting at a reasonable speed, he led us out of the storage room and down a corridor to a battered old desk by a set of double garage-type doors. Mr. Clark explained that the desk was his and that this part of the building was a loading dock.

Meanwhile, Hooligan sat himself down and looked up expectantly. As far as he was concerned, this was the finish line, he had won the race and now he wanted his prize.

I said, "Good puppy!" and pulled a doggy treat from my pocket and gave it to him.

Mr. Clark said, "There's a driveway and a ramp outside for delivery trucks, but it's not as big as the new one, so it's not used much anymore. Sometimes I think everybody upstairs"—he looked at Professor Rexington—"has forgotten us."

Tessa folded her arms across her chest like she always does when she's interviewing a witness. "Mr. Clark, do you keep track of what's delivered here?"

Mr. Clark looked offended. "That's my job." He pulled a fat black binder out of his desk. "What day are you interested in?"

Tessa said Friday morning, and Mr. Clark turned a couple of pages. "Is it this one?" he asked. "One of my coworkers entered it. I don't work Friday mornings."

The entry read: "Received 11:55 a.m., from Red Heart Delivery, one wooden crate weighing 15 pounds, 4 ounces. Destination 8th floor, office of Professor Rexington."

"Jackpot, Cammie!" Tessa said.

"Yeah, whaddya know?" Nate said. "Your plan actually worked."

"It's Hooligan who should get the credit," I said modestly. But actually I was pretty proud. Now all we had to do was phone Red Heart Delivery, find out who had sent the crate and bingo—we had cracked the case of the missing dinosaur egg!

CHAPTER TWELVE

We thanked Mr. Clark and Professor Rexington and said good-bye. Then Malik drove us back to the White House. On the way, I slipped our secret weapon one more doggy treat. He deserved it.

At home, we wanted to look up Red Heart Delivery right away and call, but we were already late for dinner. Mom, Dad and Aunt Jen were busy, so we kids were supposed to eat with Granny in the Family Kitchen—and she likes to eat at six-thirty sharp.

We had tuna casserole with noodles and peas, which maybe doesn't sound that delicious, but there were fried bread crumbs on top, and homemade applesauce, too. When Granny gets sick of being waited on by the White House staff, she likes to cook for us.

While we ate, we took turns telling her what had happened at the museum. When we were done, she said, "I just have one question. You found the crumpled newspaper the egg was packed in—"

"It was dated Thursday, April sixth," said Nate. "We made sure to check."

Granny nodded. "Good...and what newspaper was it?"

Tessa, Nate and I looked at each other. None of us had noticed—and we should have—*duh*. The town the newspaper came from might tell us the town the ostrich egg came from!

Granny saw we felt dumb, so she tried an easier question. "Was the newspaper written in English?"

I thought for a second. "Yes, because I could read the date."

Granny nodded. "In that case, it didn't come from a certain nearby nation. They don't speak English there."

"So President Manfred Alfredo-Chin couldn't have packed the ostrich egg," I said. "He must not be the thief...unless he has helpers in an English-speaking place."

"We already know Professor Bohn is the thief, Cammie," Tessa said. "And when we call Red Heart Delivery, we're going to find out that Professor Bohn's the one who sent the egg."

I didn't think so.

And I was right.

But for all the wrong reasons.

After we put the dishes in the dishwasher, we went up to Nate's room on the third floor to use his computer. He looked all over the Web, but he couldn't find Red Heart Delivery anywhere.

So we trooped back downstairs to find Granny, who was reading in the West Sitting Hall, and she got up and looked till she found an old paper phone book in a drawer in the Family Kitchen.

There was no Red Heart Delivery there, either.

"Maybe they don't want publicity," Tessa said.

"All businesses want publicity," Granny said. "Otherwise, how do they get customers?"

"Then why can't we find them?" Nate asked.

"Only one reason I can think of," said Granny. "Because they don't exist."

"Well, *that's* disappointing!" Tessa said.

"A dead end." I sighed. "What do we do now?"

Granny shrugged. "When you come to a dead end, you try another direction."

And the next day, Monday, that's just what I did.

CHAPTER THIRTEEN

I'm in fifth grade, and Monday is the day fifth graders have library after lunch.

For our investigation, this turned out to be lucky, because Mr. Brackbill, the school librarian, likes to give us Internet research assignments.

That day the assignment was: Find five dinosaur facts from five reliable websites.

Dinosaur facts—*yes!*

Even better, we were allowed to pick our own partners, and right away I looked around for Evgenia. She is one of those quiet kinds of people you don't notice till one day she says something that is seriously smart.

"I have an idea for what to research," I said as soon as we sat down at the computer table. "Not that long ago, a dinosaur egg fossil was found in a certain nearby nation. Let's look that up. I mean"—I suddenly realized that might sound bossy—"unless you have a better idea."

Evgenia grinned as she logged us in to the computer. "You're detecting again, aren't you? When Jan and Larry talked about that missing egg last week? I thought, 'That sounds exactly like a job for the First Kids!'"

We started by searching "dinosaur egg" and the name of the certain nearby nation. Bingo—we got lots of results from science magazines, newspapers, museums and TV stations. One of them included both Professor Rexington and Professor Bohn, so we tried that one first, and...guess what?

We found out the two paleontologists don't like each other at all!

It's not because of personal stuff. It's because of science. I didn't understand everything in the article, but basically they disagree about whether the dinosaur that laid the missing egg is a close relative of birds that live today. Professor Bohn thinks it is, and Professor Rexington thinks it's not.

I guess if you're a scientist, you think this kind of stuff is worth fighting about.

Anyway, the reason the dinosaur egg was coming to the United States at all was so Professor Rexington and Professor Bohn could study the shell. Each one thought its structure would prove he—or she—was right.

Evgenia and I looked at some more websites and found a picture of the missing dinosaur egg. I couldn't help thinking the scientists who found it had to have been pretty smart even to have recognized that a gray, oval-shaped rock was really an egg fossil.

Mr. Brackbill would give us extra credit for having

a picture, so I copied and pasted it into my document. Then I typed these facts:

- The egg was found last fall by Professor Rexington, Professor Bohn and a team of scientists from the nearby nation.
- It probably came from a dinosaur called Unenlagia that was probably about six feet tall and had feathers.
- The Unenlagia dinosaur could flap its front legs the way birds flap their wings.
- "Unenlagia" means "half-bird" in a South American language.

We still needed another fact, and Evgenia saw that there was an article about the egg on the website of a certain nearby nation. Luckily, it was written in English, but what it said was totally different from the other ones:

The American scientists who found this so-called dinosaur egg are mistaken. Their ignorance can be seen very easily by the fact that they recently mistook an ostrich egg for a dinosaur egg at a presentation at an important museum in the capital of the United States of America.

In fact, the so-called dinosaur egg discovered in our nation last year belonged to a large bird that has been extinct for one century only. As every schoolchild in our nation knows, no animal or plant life lived within our borders until long after the time of the dinosaurs.

Evgenia's eyes got big. "This is totally the opposite of everything else we've been reading!"

"And it isn't very nice about Professor Bohn and Professor Rexington, either," I said.

"Mr. Brackbill says just because you find something on the Internet doesn't make it true," Evgenia said. "You have to cross-check and consider sources."

"I guess he's right," I said. "Let's look up when the Unenlagia dinosaur lived."

Evgenia went back to the Smithsonian website and found the answer. Then she added:

- Unenlagia lived in the Mesozoic period, about 90 million years ago.

I couldn't wait to tell Nate and Tessa what I had learned, so of course the rest of the school day passed extra slowly. Finally, at 3:15, I was set free. Jeremy was driving the van that met us out front. Granny was in back.

I started explaining about the library before I was even buckled in. When I was finished, Nate said, "Good job, Cameron! Now we know why Professor Bohn stole the egg. He wanted to keep it away from Professor Rexington."

Uh-oh. I never thought of that! I started to argue, but Granny interrupted with news of her own.

"Since you children were busy in school, I did a little

detecting myself." Granny knows all about detecting. She used to be a police officer. "That newspaper in Professor Rexington's wastebasket? It was the *Washington Post*. So it seems whoever sent the ostrich egg must have packed it up right here in town."

Tessa grinned. "Good job, Granny! Mr. Morgan and Mr. Webb will be super proud. They've only been gone since yesterday, and already we've gathered two pieces of evidence to help prove it was Professor Bohn who stole the dinosaur egg."

CHAPTER FOURTEEN

What was I doing wrong?

Solving the case was supposed to prove Professor Bohn was innocent. But so far it seemed more like the opposite.

I needed to think. So after Tessa, Nate and I had eaten our snack, I asked Granny if she thought Mr. Bryant would let me take Hooligan for a walk around the South Lawn.

Mr. Bryant used to operate the Presidential Elevator, but now he works for our family, taking care of Hooligan on weekdays.

"I'm sure Mr. Bryant will be happy for the coffee break," Granny said. "But Charlotte will have to go with you."

"I know," I said.

"And we'll have to alert the other officers outside."

"I know."

"And mind the public, Cameron. Don't talk to anybody—and remember, they're all voters or potential voters."

When Granny said "the public," she meant the people outside the White House fence looking in. I'm not supposed to actually talk to these people, because I might say something dumb by mistake that would get on the news and be embarrassing. On the other hand, I should always smile and be polite, because if I don't, people might not vote for Mom.

"I know, Granny. I am a representative of the family."

Granny smiled, then reached over and gave my shoulder a squeeze. "Living in the White House is a bother sometimes, Cameron. But there are a lot of privileges, too. You're looking forward to the Easter egg roll, aren't you?"

An Easter egg roll is a race where you push a hard-boiled egg with a spoon. The tradition started at the White House way back in the 1800s, and now thousands of people come to the South Lawn the day after Easter to celebrate. There are games and music and food—kind of like a church picnic, only bigger.

I nodded. "I'm looking forward to the fried rice, too," I said, which made Granny laugh. The first time Tessa ever heard of an Easter egg roll, she thought it was Chinese food.

While Granny got hold of Charlotte and Mr. Bryant, I went to Tessa's and my bedroom to put on jeans and sneakers. Then I read over my notes for the case so they'd be fresh in my mind.

On my way downstairs, I stopped by Hooligan's room. Tessa was there, sitting on the floor by the kittens—two orange, one black, and three gray tabbies—a squirming mass of fur and cuteness. I reached in and tickled the mama, who flicked her tail but didn't bother to wake up.

"The kitten book says they'll be more fun next week when they can see and hear," Tessa said. "But they'll be messier, too. Right now the mama cleans up most of the disgusting parts."

I said, "No wonder she's tired." Then I told Tessa I was going out to walk Hooligan and think.

"About the case?" she asked.

I nodded.

"You don't think Professor Bohn stole the egg, do you?"

"It's obvious, huh?"

"*Hello-o-o?* I'm your *sister*! But we don't get to pick who did it, Cammie. Like Granny says, we have to be fair and look at the evidence."

"I'm trying," I said. "But the truth is, I'd rather it was somebody else—like Professor Rexington. She's not nearly as nice. And she has a motive, too, right? She wants the egg as much as Professor Bohn does. She wants to prove she's the one who's right about birds and dinosaurs."

Tessa said, "I wasn't going to tell you this, but I thought of something else. Why did Professor Rexington recycle the crate so fast?"

I shrugged. "Because she's super well organized? You saw how tidy her office was."

"Maybe," said Tessa, "or maybe because the crate had a return address or some other clue. Maybe there was something she didn't want us to see."

I stared at my sister. "I should've thought of that!"

Tessa said, "Why? Because you're older?"

"No, because I'm smarter—*duh*." And then I had to move fast because Tessa was scrambling to her feet, ready to pound me.

CHAPTER FIFTEEN

I got away from my sister okay.

All I had to do was call over my shoulder, "I take it back! You're smart, too!" then run down two flights of stairs and cross into the Diplomatic Reception Room, which is how you get to the South Lawn.

Mr. Bryant and Charlotte met me under the awning outside, and Mr. Bryant handed me Hooligan's leash.

"I appreciate your taking over for a few minutes, Cameron. Your grandmother is putting on a pot of coffee." Then he gave Hooligan a pat on the head. "You behave yourself. Understand?"

Hooligan answered by sitting politely and displaying his most noble profile.

Charlotte rolled her eyes. "Sometimes I think this dog should travel with his personal photographer."

"Yeah," I said, "he has a lot in common with my sister that way."

"Where shall we walk?" Charlotte asked after Mr. Bryant left to go meet Granny.

I said, "Children's Garden," which is a part of the South Lawn that has a path and a pond and a climbing tree. A First Lady a long time ago had it built for when her grandchildren came to visit.

Charlotte and I turned right toward the West Wing, where my mom's office is. Nearing it, I saw her and a cluster of other people walking in the Rose Garden. Right away, I noticed one of the men because he wasn't wearing a suit like everybody else. Instead, he had on an untucked, short-sleeve white shirt and black pants. . . .

Wait a sec. Hadn't there been a guy at Professor Bohn's museum talk in a shirt like that?

I pointed him out to Charlotte, who told me that kind of shirt is called a guayabera—pronounced "gwy-uh-bear-uh"—and they're popular in countries where it's hot.

"Who are those guys, anyway?" I asked her.

Charlotte squinted at them. "I'm not sure. Foreign dignitaries, I guess."

A foreign dignitary is somebody important who comes from another country. Before I could ask where these ones were from, I got distracted by Hooligan, who had stopped to sniff the air.

Uh-oh.

This could be trouble.

I got a good grip on his leash . . . but not good enough, because half a second later he bolted for the Rose Garden, tugging me off-balance and yanking the leash out of my hand.

"Hooligan!" I tried to call, but only the first syl-

lable came out. The second two were muted by the combination of grass and earth my face encountered on the ground—*owieee!*

"Cammie, are you okay?" Charlotte reached down to help me. I wiped the dirt out of my eyes and saw Hooligan was on a collision course with Mom and the foreign dignitaries.

Charlotte cringed. "I hope they're from a friendly country."

Me, too, because by now, Hooligan had zeroed in on his intended target—none other than the man in the guayabera shirt—and was gathering himself to make a leap.

The man must not have been expecting a big, furry, flying impact, because—*pow!*—when Hooligan connected—*ouch!*—he toppled over backward.

"Oh, dear," I said, "I hope that guy likes dogs."

CHAPTER SIXTEEN

The guy did not like dogs.

Especially big dogs that jump on you, knock you over and slobber on your face.

But it's not like he had to go to the hospital or anything.

And Mom said the White House laundry might be able to wash the paw prints out if he didn't mind handing over his shirt.

There are always newspeople at the White House, and now—as the guy was helped to his feet—their cameras whirred and clicked.

Meanwhile, my mom introduced us. "This is my daughter Cameron, Mr. Valenteen. And she is about to apologize for our dog's terrible behavior."

"I'm really sorry," I said. "I don't know why Hooligan did that. Usually he only attacks squirrels and pigeons."

"I am not a squirrel or a pigeon," Mr. Valenteen said.

"I can see that," I said.

"Good. Then we're all in agreement," said Mom.

"Cameron, I'll see you at dinner. Gentlemen? Shall we continue our discussions inside?"

Mom, Mr. Valenteen and the guys in suits turned and headed for my mom's office. Meanwhile, Hooligan sat himself down in good-dog fashion and looked up at me expectantly.

"What's with you, anyway?" I asked him. "You don't get a doggy treat for jumping on some poor, random guy. You know that, right?"

But apparently he didn't know that, because he cocked his head and woofed a sad and disappointed little *woof.*

"Was he the same man from the museum?" Charlotte asked me. "Or just wearing the same kind of shirt?"

"Same man," I said. "Weird, huh? I guess he must be interested in dinosaurs."

We turned toward the Children's Garden, and I asked Charlotte if she'd mind helping me go over the evidence.

"Happy to," she said. "After all, I am a law enforcement professional. What do you know so far?"

Since I had just reviewed my notes, it was easy to tell her the important parts:

- Jan and Larry said the dinosaur egg might be missing because of politics in a certain nearby nation.
- Professor Bohn was the "unnamed source" who told them that.

- The crate had been scanned in at Dulles airport on Thursday.
- The packing newspaper was the *Washington Post*, dated last Thursday.
- The delivery company, Red Heart, didn't exist.
- Professor Rexington and Professor Bohn were in a feud about the family history of dinosaurs and birds.

By this time we had passed the tennis courts and gone under the trellis into the garden, which is surrounded by trees and bushes. A path leads to the goldfish pond, and children and grandchildren of past presidents have left their handprints in the concrete paving stones. I hopscotched over the names "Jenna Bush" and "Barbara Bush," then sat down in one of the white metal chairs by the pond.

Instead of checking out the goldfish, Hooligan lay down next to me and closed his eyes. It must be hard work, attacking foreign dignitaries.

"Mr. Morgan and Mr. Webb say Professor Bohn is the thief, but I'm not sure," I told Charlotte. "Maybe instead, the egg's disappearance is connected to a certain nearby nation."

"That's where Mr. Valenteen is from," Charlotte said. "I only realized it when I saw the dignitaries close-up. With all the prodemocracy protests there, they want your mom to reaffirm the U.S.'s alliance with President Manfred Alfredo-Chin."

"What does that mean—reaffirm the alliance?" I asked.

"Tell all the other countries the United States still likes him," Charlotte said.

I thought for a second. "So it's the same as when my best friend, Courtney Lozana, ate the last cookie out of my lunch? And I got mad, but the next day she gave me a bag of chips and told me to tell all our other friends how I wasn't mad at her anymore so they wouldn't be mad at her, either?"

Charlotte looked thoughtful. "Pretty much, yeah. Sometimes countries act a lot like fifth graders. But none of that is helping you with your case. I have a question. Maybe you said, but I missed it. Where did that ostrich egg come from?"

For a second, I felt annoyed. Usually I like Charlotte, because even though I'm a kid, she listens to me. But now it was like she hadn't heard me at all. "From the crate at the museum and before that from Red Heart Delivery," I repeated.

"Yeah, yeah, I got all that," Charlotte said. "But *before* that. The egg was ready to hatch, so it probably came from nearby. There can't be that many places to get an ostrich egg around here. So maybe if you found the place where the egg was laid?"

I sat still for a moment, listening to the pond burble and watching a tan cardinal and her red boyfriend doing a jig by its edge. Then I said, "Charlotte, you're a genius."

CHAPTER SEVENTEEN

Charlotte was not only a genius. She was right. There aren't many places around Washington to get an ostrich egg. In fact, there is only one: Mega Bird Farm, located in the country about thirty miles from the White House.

That was the result that came back when Nate went online and entered "ostrich farm Washington D.C." into the search engine right before dinner.

"I'll call them!" Tessa volunteered. She always likes to do the talking.

"You can give it a try," I said. "Ask them if—"

"I *know* what to ask, Cammie." Tessa had already picked up the phone on Nate's desk and was dialing the number on the website. After a few seconds, she said, "Hello? This is Tessa Parks, and...yes, that Tessa Parks, and...yes, I am totally serious."

I didn't have to hear the other side of the conversation to imagine it. A lot of times when one of us calls somebody we don't know, they don't believe we're really us.

"Thank you," Tessa went on. "I think she's a good president, too. Anyway, my sister and my cousin and I are investigating a case, and we have some questions for you.... Uh, hold on a sec, would you?" Tessa looked up at me and Nate. "What are our questions, again?"

"Ask if somebody bought an egg last week," Nate said.

"And if somebody did buy an egg, who was it?" I said.

Tessa repeated the questions, listened and nodded. "Oh, really? Okay, I'll check.... And you have a very mega day, too!" She hung up.

"Well?" Nate and I said at the same time.

"She doesn't like to give information out over the phone," Tessa said. "But I should still have a very mega day."

"So we have to go out there?" I said.

Tessa grinned and pumped her fist. *"Road trip!"*

A road trip sounded good to me, too. The problem was that when you're the president's kid, a road trip is not so easy. The Secret Service would have to go with us and they would have to scout the place in advance. Since they have other things to do, arrangements might take a while. The question was, how long?

At dinner, we told Granny we wanted to visit Mega Bird Farm, and she agreed it was a good idea. After dinner, she called to talk to the Secret Service about how soon we could go. Tessa, Nate and I were finishing our homework in the solarium when Charlotte came in to deliver the bad news.

"Friday after school?" Tessa waved her arms the way she does. "But what will we tell Mr. Morgan and Mr. Webb? They are going to be *so-o-o* disappointed!"

"I thought of that," Charlotte said, "so I got in touch with them already. They're having such a good time in Pittsburgh, they've decided to stay a few more days. But they said don't worry, and they promise to call when they get back."

CHAPTER EIGHTEEN

A lot of times I am surprised by the stuff the news guys think is important. For example, remember when Hooligan knocked over that foreign dignitary—Mr. Valenteen?

That was on Monday afternoon, and for the rest of the week, it was like you couldn't turn on the TV or look at the Web without seeing Hooligan leaping, the guy's face looking scared and unhappy, and then Hooligan again—showing off his profile like he was proud he had knocked somebody over.

As you can imagine, this was all pretty embarrassing for my mom and the rest of the United States government.

So on Thursday when Tessa's and my friend Toni called to invite us and Nate and Hooligan over to her house, my mom was happy. In case you don't remember, Toni's father is the ambassador from Mr. Valenteen's nation. According to Mom, the invitation was supposed to be a sign that the people there were ready to forgive Hooligan and the American people.

Tessa disagreed. "I don't think the invitation is a sign of anything," she said. "I think Toni just invited us because we're friends. Plus Toni told me there's this cool new rock in her rock collection and she wants us to see it."

The invitation was for Easter after lunch. Toni's family lives in the ambassador's house, which is next to the office part of the embassy in the neighborhood of Washington, D.C. called Georgetown. Hooligan was included because he's friends with Toni's dog, Ozzabelle. While we checked out the rocks, they were going to have a playdate.

Besides the invitation from Toni, a few other things happened that week:

- I studied my spelling words for the Friday test and did math homework.
- Tessa and I tried on our Easter dresses to make sure they fit.
- The kittens opened their eyes the rest of the way.
- Tessa, Nate, the Easter Bunny and I assembled baskets to be given as prizes at the Easter egg roll. (The Easter Bunny was really one of my mom's staffers dressed up in a costume he told us was hot and itchy.)
- We got a postcard from Mr. Morgan and Mr. Webb. It showed a picture of a big, swoopy bridge over

the Ohio River, and it said: "Happy Detecting! See you next week!"

Finally it was Friday, and after school Granny and Charlotte picked us up in one of the White House vans.

Malik drove, and we went northwest out of the city into Maryland. For the first part, the scenery was mostly office buildings, but after a while we were in the country—big houses and rolling green hills with pink-flowering trees and red-flowering bushes.

Tessa fell asleep.

Nate asked, "Are we there yet?"

After we left the highway we drove on back roads for a while till we rounded a bend and saw a sign that read MEGA BIRD FARM.

I elbowed Tessa, who opened her eyes, looked out the window and squealed: "Are those for real?"

CHAPTER NINETEEN

Yes, Tessa, they were for real—a flock of about fifty ostriches jogging alongside the van as it wound its way up a steep and curving driveway. I was glad the ostriches were on the other side of a chain-link fence.

Charlotte said they looked like long-legged feather dusters, and Nate said they looked like they had snakes for necks.

I thought they for sure looked a lot more like dinosaurs than they did like Granny's canary, or a cardinal, or any other normal bird.

At the end of the driveway was a one-story blue building with a covered porch and a sign on the door that said OPEN. Malik pulled into a parking space in front, and we all climbed out. An SUV was there already. It didn't have writing on it or anything, but I knew it belonged to the Secret Service. Some agents would have come out ahead of us just to make sure things were okay. Now they were hanging around nearby but out of sight.

The door of the blue building opened, and a smiling woman with frizzy gray hair came out. "Welcome! I'm Nancy Aviano, and most of you I recognize from the TV. It's Tessa I spoke to on the phone, correct?"

"*Correct-amento!*" said Tessa. She introduced Granny, Charlotte, Malik and me, and we all shook hands.

"I know you have some questions," Nancy Aviano said, "but first can I show you around?"

"Yes, please!" said Tessa. "I have never in my life met a grown-up ostrich before."

Mrs. Aviano turned out to be the same amount chatty as she was nice. Luckily, ostriches are interesting, so we didn't mind listening...and listening.

First she led us over to the fence so we could look at the ostriches and they could look back at us. From my bird book, I already knew a lot of what Mrs. Aviano was saying—how ostriches are native to Africa, run forty-five miles per hour and live as long as fifty years.

But reading a book isn't the same as seeing something close-up. Ostriches are awesome! They have huge eyes and long eyelashes, so their faces look friendly even if the rest of them looks weird. They're bigger than NBA players, up to nine feet tall and 350 pounds. They're super curious. One tried to peck Granny's bracelet, and another went for Charlotte's watch.

"They won't hurt you," Mrs. Aviano said, "unless you scare them. If they feel threatened, they kick, and I'm here to tell you that big toenail packs a wallop."

Next Mrs. Aviano showed us the barn where the ostriches are fed, and the shed she uses as a nursery.

Inside, there were heated boxes called incubators for the eggs, and bigger boxes called brooders for the young chicks. The older chicks had a separate room. They were clumsy and funny and covered with downy, spotted feathers that looked more like fur.

"*Awww,*" Tessa said. "I wish we could've kept Dino. I bet Hooligan would've loved him."

"Hooligan probably would have tried to beat up on Dino when he was a chick," Nate said. "Then what a surprise when Dino grew up and wanted revenge!"

Mrs. Aviano asked who Dino was, and how was Hooligan, anyway? Like everyone else in America, she had seen our dog on TV plenty of times. As we walked back to the office, we explained how Hooligan really is good—he just has too much energy.

Then Tessa said, "And Dino is the reason we're here. Cammie, do you have your notebook?"

I held it up. "I'm ready."

Inside, Mrs. Aviano settled into her desk chair, and Tessa crossed her arms over her chest like she always does when she's going to ask questions.

Only, the way it turned out, she didn't even have to.

CHAPTER TWENTY

"You know," Mrs. Aviano began before Tessa had said a word, "you're not the only ones who want to know about that egg. A black-haired lady came out earlier in the week with the same question, and I told her what I'm going to tell you, namely that I never got the fellow's name because he paid cash.

"He showed up last Thursday without phoning ahead. He wanted an egg that had already been incubated, he said. It was an unusual request, but he assured me he'd be able to take care of the chick."

Tessa said, "Do you remember—"

"What he looked like? Average height. Average face. Average age. Now, if he'd been an ostrich, then I'd've paid more attention to details."

Tessa tried again. "What about—"

"The black-haired lady?" Mrs. Aviano shrugged. "She was out here the day before yesterday—Wednesday—and I would call her average-looking. Oh—but she had an accent. A foreign accent. And she told me her name—"

"Yes?" said Tessa.

"—but I forgot it."

By now, our visit to Mega Bird Farm was reminding me of our visit to the museum with Hooligan—interesting but a detecting dead end.

And Tessa was frustrated enough that she actually asked for help. "Can you guys think of anything?" She looked at me and Nate.

I shrugged, but Nate said, "Mrs. Aviano, you don't happen to have security cameras, do you? Video cameras?"

"Are you kidding?" said Mrs. Aviano. "A breeding pair of ostriches is worth a hundred thousand dollars! Of course we've got security cameras! You wanna see video of those visitors? Heck—why didn't you say so?"

The video playback was on the computer, so Tessa, Nate and I gathered around Mrs. Aviano's desk to watch. Setting everything up, Mrs. Aviano explained that the cameras only turn on when something moves near them. Because of that, there isn't that much video, and it only took about two seconds to find what we wanted.

The video shot Wednesday morning showed a lady with black hair standing at the counter in the office. When Mrs. Aviano paused the video, Tessa said, "Zoom in so we can see her face."

"Please," I added.

Mrs. Aviano tapped a key, and the lady's face filled

the screen. It was a little blurry, but you could tell she was probably older than my mom or Aunt Jen, and she had pale skin, a straight nose and small eyes. Her black hair was short. She was frowning.

None of us had ever seen her before, and neither—when we called her over to look—had Charlotte.

Next Mrs. Aviano pulled up the video from the day the average-looking man bought the egg. There was footage of him at the counter in the office, too, but the best picture was one in the incubator room. When Mrs. Aviano zoomed in, we all gasped, and Mrs. Aviano said, "Now that I look at him again, he does seem kind of familiar."

"Yeah, he does," said Tessa. "He's been on TV approximately one zillion times since Hooligan knocked him over in the Rose Garden on Monday. His name is Mr. Valenteen, and he's a foreign dignitary from a certain nearby nation."

CHAPTER TWENTY-ONE

In the van on the way back to the White House, Tessa waved her arms and announced: "The case is solved. Mr. Valenteen did it!"

Granny said, *"Hmmm,"* and the way she said *"Hmmm,"* you could tell it meant "or not."

Tessa scowled. "What?"

"You're right that Mr. Valenteen must have delivered the ostrich egg to the museum," Granny said. "In fact, I think you may also have solved the mystery of why Hooligan knocked him over in the Rose Garden. Either the egg smelled like Mr. Valenteen—or Mr. Valenteen smelled like the egg."

"Oh, so that's why Hooligan expected a reward!" I said.

"And I thought of something, too," said Nate. "The name of the delivery company was Red Heart, right? Like Valentine's Day?"

Tessa smacked her forehead. *"Duh!* So Mr. *Valenteen*'s the one who invented the delivery company that doesn't exist!"

Granny nodded. "You've done a solid job on the ostrich egg. But you still don't know what happened to the egg that matters, the dinosaur egg."

Shoot. As usual, Granny was right.

"We know Professor Rexington and Professor Bohn found it in a certain nearby nation," I said. "And we know their colleagues there shipped it to the United States. Then, according to Mr. Morgan and Mr. Webb, it arrived at the airport here....And after that, it disappeared."

"Right," said Granny. "So where is it?"

Tessa, Nate and I looked at each other. We had no idea.

"Besides that," Granny said, "as far as we know, Mr. Morgan and Mr. Webb are still convinced the real thief is Professor Bohn."

"Maybe there's a connection we don't know about between Professor Bohn and Mr. Valenteen," Nate said.

"And what about the lady with black hair?" Granny asked. "How is she connected?"

"She must not know Mr. Valenteen, anyway," I said. "Because if she did, she would've known he bought the ostrich egg, and she wouldn't have gone to Mega Bird Farm to ask."

Granny said, "I have another thought. There are two sides to the political troubles in a certain nearby nation— the prodemocracy side that wants new elections, and President Alfredo-Chin's side that doesn't. What if the lady and Mr. Valenteen are on opposite sides?"

"Which side is Mr. Valenteen on?" Tessa asked.

"President Manfred Alfredo-Chin's—*duh*," said

Nate, "because he works for President Chin's embassy here in Washington."

Malik piped up from the driver's seat: "I know some-one on the prodemocracy side."

Charlotte was riding shotgun. "Who's that?"

Instead of answering, Malik pressed some buttons on the dashboard music player, and a song came on. It had a good beat but lame, lovey-dovey lyrics. Nate stuck a finger down his throat, but then—to my horror—Granny started singing along:

Lina is gone,
The woman is gone.
Left a note on my door,
Couldn't take any more....

We kids all looked at each other. This had to stop. Granny was totally embarrassing herself in front of Charlotte and Malik!

I opened my mouth to say something—but before I could, Charlotte and Malik solved the problem. They started singing, too!

Lina is gone,
The woman is gone.
A fool always fails
And ends in love's jail....

I tried hard to pretend I was somewhere else. Then I

realized I recognized the song. It was one my dad used to play when I was little.

"Hey—isn't that Eb Ghanamamma?" I said.

Malik grinned at me in the rearview mirror, then—still singing—nudged Charlotte and nodded at the glove compartment. Charlotte opened it and pulled out an old, beat-up CD case, which she handed back to Tessa and me.

The title was *Lina and Other Loves*, and on the front was a picture of Eb Ghanamamma himself—curly black hair, dark eyes, a crooked nose and a skinny face. His expression was what Mom would call "pouty."

Eb Ghanamamma, in case you don't know, is a famous folk singer from a certain nearby nation. Like Malik said, he is also one of the protesters against the government of President Manfred Alfredo-Chin. I know that because—even though we have never actually met—Eb Ghanamamma helped Tessa, Nate and me solve the Case of the Diamond Dog Collar.

Malik was turning the van into the White House's East Gate when Granny looked over her shoulder at us and said, "So by now it should be obvious what your next move is."

Tessa nodded. "Totally obvious! Go ahead, Cammie. Tell her."

"Uh...I would if I knew. Nate?"

My cousin shook his head. "For once, there is something I don't know. What's our next move, Granny?"

"You're going to visit Toni Alfredo-Chin at the embassy on Sunday anyway," Granny said. "What if we make an appointment for you to interview Mr. Valenteen at the same time?"

CHAPTER TWENTY-TWO

Granny made a phone call.

The appointment was set for three o'clock Sunday at the embassy.

After that it was time for dinner. And guess what—something unusual and amazing happened: Tessa and I got to eat with both our parents! More amazing yet, after dinner, we all watched a movie together.

It was a lot like being a normal family...except the food was cooked by the White House chef and served by a butler. And the movie was a brand-new Disney one screened in the private White House theater.

Before bed, we played Monopoly in the solarium. Monopoly is a family tradition on Friday nights, but a lot of times Mom is too busy.

In case you're wondering, the whole time, we hardly talked about the missing dinosaur egg. Nate was with his mom, and Tessa's and my brains needed a break.

What we talked about instead were relaxing topics—

like world peace and pollution and whether the old Disney movies are better than the new ones.

Mom won at Monopoly, which was good because she is a grumpy loser. The rule is loser puts the game away, which is what Tessa and I were doing when Mom's phone rang. She listened, frowned, shrugged and said, "Okay, then. We'll find out more tomorrow, I guess."

When she hung up, she looked at Tessa and me.

"What?" we asked at the same time.

"I am sorry to report that your interview with Mr. Valenteen has been canceled. It seems President Alfredo-Chin has asked him to return home. About an hour ago, he left on a plane bound for the capital of a certain nearby nation."

Can I tell you a secret?

I wasn't that upset that the interview was canceled. With Easter on Sunday and the egg roll on Monday, my family had a lot going on.

Maybe Tessa, Nate and I could just chill until Mr. Morgan and Mr. Webb came back from Pittsburgh. Didn't we already have enough to report?

After we got into bed and turned the lights out, I confessed this to Tessa.

She said, "You're right, Cammie. Mr. Morgan and Mr. Webb probably got the rest of the evidence they need in Pittsburgh, anyway. And now they'll be able to prove it was Professor Bohn all along."

"Wait!" I rolled over. "No! Not Professor Bohn—Mr. Valenteen! Or maybe Professor Rexington."

"Okay, fine," Tessa said, "but you know what Aunt Jen says: 'If you want something done right, you have to do it yourself.'"

I sighed. "So you're saying we don't get the weekend off?"

It was dark in our room, but from the way her sheets rustled, I knew my sister was getting all dramatic the way she does. "What I'm *saying* is: Don't worry about a thing because—lucky for you—I am about to hatch a foolproof plan!"

CHAPTER TWENTY-THREE

There was no time to talk about plans on Saturday morning. As usual, Granny took Tessa to ballet, and Dad went with me to my soccer game. I play for the D.C. Destroyers, and that day we got D.C. Destroyed.

Luckily, unlike some people I could mention, I am not a grumpy loser.

Granny made us sandwiches for lunch. We ate in the Family Kitchen. This was the first chance Tessa and I had had to tell Nate that the interview with Mr. Valenteen had been canceled.

"No worries, though," said Tessa. "I have a foolproof plan!"

"What is it?"

"I'll tell you tomorrow," Tessa said. "Right now, it still needs time to incubate."

"Very funny," said Nate.

Tessa giggled. "I know. Sometimes I crack myself up. Get it?"

When lunch was over, Nate went upstairs to meet

his math tutor. Aunt Jen says Nate's not challenged by fifth-grade math, so he's learning trigonometry. Did I mention how it's lucky Aunt Jen isn't my mom? Meanwhile, I was thinking I might invite my friend Courtney to come over and go bowling—the White House has its own bowling alley—but before I could, Mom came in.

"Mama!" Tessa hopped up and hugged her around the waist. "Are you taking the afternoon off to play with us?"

"I wish I could," Mom said. "But actually, I'm here because Ms. Ann Major has a project, and she needs your help."

Ms. Ann Major is a deputy assistant press secretary on my mom's staff. We know her because her beagle, Pickles, went to obedience school with Hooligan.

"What project?" I asked.

"Ms. Major wants to help us make sure the news guys cover your visit to Toni's house tomorrow," Mom said. "If they do, it will be good for the friendship between our government and President Alfredo-Chin's."

"I'm confused, Mama," Tessa said. "Eb Ghanamamma doesn't like President Alfredo-Chin, right? And Eb Ghanamamma wants democracy. Don't we want democracy, too?"

"Of course we do," Mom said, "but not just yet."

"So what does Ms. Major want us to do?" Tessa asked.

Mom looked at her watch. "Meet her at her desk in ten minutes, and she'll tell you."

* * *

Ms. Major's desk is in a maze of cubicles in the West Wing—which is a building next to the house part of the White House. You get there through a special kind of hallway called a colonnade. Charlotte came, too, and the three of us scrunched into chairs.

The project turned out to be a short video about Tessa's and my friendship with Toni. Right now, Ms. Major wanted us to talk about how great Toni is in front of a camera. Tomorrow at the embassy, somebody would record more footage. Then Ms. Major would edit the clips together for the Web and TV.

If we were lucky, Jan and Larry might even show it.

Tessa said, *"Yes!"* and I said, "Do I have to?"

Ms. Major laughed at me. "It will be painless, I promise."

"Only"—Tessa frowned down at her clothes—"I look like a *wreck!*"

"You both look fine," Ms. Major said. "Come on outside."

We went out to the Rose Garden, where Ms. Major sat Tessa and me down in patio chairs, told us to act natural and aimed the video camera. Tessa straightened her shoulders, tossed her blond curls, flashed her teeth and told the camera who Toni is, how we gave her a puppy named Ozzabelle, and how she is just the greatest friend ever.

I sat like a lump until Ms. Major said, "Cameron? I'm sure you don't realize it, but you're scowling."

I said, "That wasn't a scowl. *This* is a scowl," and showed her.

Ms. Major laughed. "Okay, how about this? Think about successfully solving a mystery."

I must have smiled then, because Ms. Major said, "Better." Then she asked me to tell how we met Toni, and I did, and then—at last—we were done.

Ms. Major had been right. It wasn't that bad. But one thing was for sure. No way was I ever going to watch the finished product.

CHAPTER TWENTY-FOUR

I had been wondering if Easter morning in the White House would be a lot different than Easters in our old house in Northwest Washington.

There were a couple of differences. The main one was that Granny, Aunt Jen and Nate hadn't lived with us back then, so the celebration was bigger now. Also, in the White House, my Easter basket was hidden in an unusual and historic place: under the big bed in the Lincoln Bedroom.

Other than that, Tessa and I put on new dresses, went to church, sang "Alleluia," came home, and ate French toast for brunch—just like we always had.

After brunch, Tessa, Nate and I changed out of our church clothes to go visit Toni. We were going early so we would be back in plenty of time for Easter dinner, which would be served downstairs in the big dining room.

All this time, Tessa still hadn't told me and Nate her plan. But when she got dressed, she put on the pink spangled ball cap she wears for detecting. Then, when we were finally leaving, she said, "Got your notebook, Cammie? You're going to need it."

The embassy of a certain nearby nation is in an old brick building in Georgetown, about fifteen minutes from the White House. There is a curlicued black metal fence around the building. In the front is a door leading to offices, and around a corner is a door that goes to the residence, where Toni and her family live.

When Malik pulled the van up to the curb, there were already white TV trucks parked there and news guys with cameras and microphones clustered on the sidewalk.

Hooligan was in the back of our van, so I walked around, opened his crate, attached his leash to his collar and let him out. It was Tessa's job to carry an Easter basket the White House pastry chef had prepared for Toni and her family.

"Ready?" Granny looked at Tessa, me and Nate. "All right then, let's do this."

Standing on each side of the embassy gate were soldiers in dark blue uniforms and caps. They had guns on their belts and bigger guns slung over their shoulders. I smiled at one as we walked through, but he didn't smile back.

Yikes, I thought, but then I remembered that Secret Service people would be all around as long as we were inside. There was nothing to worry about—even if the soldiers from the nearby nation didn't seem so friendly.

We followed a walkway to the front door, and Granny rang the doorbell. Instantly, there was a total ruckus of hysterical yip-yip-yipping from inside.

Hooligan responded with woof-woof-woofing of his own, not to mention he pulled the leash so hard I had to brace myself. Granny offered to take it, because she's heavier, which would have been a good idea, except just then the door opened and here came Ozzabelle busting out at the same time Hooligan tried to bust in and—*bam!*—there was a drooling, fur-flying doggy collision.

Meanwhile, the leash dropped and—a few spins and tumbles later—both dogs were racing in circles around the brick courtyard while all the grown-ups either scurried out of the way or yelled or both.

In the background, I heard shouting from the news guys—"Great stuff!" "Are you getting this?"—and the whir and click of their equipment.

One thing Tessa, Nate and I have learned about doggy behavior: scurrying and yelling doesn't help. Tessa held the Easter basket up high, but besides that we just stayed out of the way and watched. Then Toni came outside and grinned at us and shouted, "Hello!"

The canine chaos was settling down—Granny had hold of Hooligan's leash, and Malik had cornered Ozzabelle—when my nose told me someone else had come out of the house, someone who smelled like perfume and cigarettes. I figured it had to be Toni's grandmother, and I turned around...and got the shock of my life.

It was the lady with black hair from the security video at Mega Bird Farm!

CHAPTER TWENTY-FIVE

My heart went *thump*, and I nudged Tessa—who looked around, too, and then so did Nate.

I don't think the lady liked how surprised we looked, because she quickly disappeared back into the house. At the same time, her frown had given me goose bumps. Was she really Toni's grandmother?

It was a few minutes before I found out. During that time, the dogs were taken to the backyard to play, and the news guys shot photos and video of my family, the Easter basket and Toni.

"Doesn't your grandmother want to be in the pictures?" Granny asked Toni.

"Oh, no." Toni shook her head. "She does not like the publicity. She says it is not her 'style.'"

Eventually, Granny and Malik left to go back to the White House. The plan was for them to return to pick us up in a couple of hours. Nate, Tessa and I followed Toni inside. In the foyer, a small, gray-haired woman greeted us with hugs—Toni's grandmother. She smelled like soap.

"It is my pleasure to meet Antonia's dear friends," she said. "And I must also take this opportunity to thank you for giving us the little dog, Ozzabelle. She is a nuisance, but she makes me laugh."

Toni's house was fancy—lots of shiny brass and black paint. Toni led us up the marble stairs to her room, which was big like Tessa's and mine. It had a bed and also a sofa, chairs and a table. I noticed the rock collection right away because it was lit up on a shelf over a desk.

Before we sat down, Toni put on some music. After a few seconds, I realized it was familiar—Eb Ghanamamma! But that couldn't be right. Wasn't Eb Ghanamamma protesting against Toni's very own uncle, President Manfred Alfredo-Chin?

I wanted to ask about that, but I was afraid it would be rude. And I wanted to ask about the lady with the black hair, too. But how was I supposed to explain where I'd seen her?

So I kept quiet.

But Tessa didn't.

"Get out your notebook, Cammie," she said as soon as we sat down. Then she straightened her detecting hat, crossed her arms over her chest and gave Toni the steely look she uses when she's questioning a suspect.

Uh-oh—was this Tessa's foolproof plan? But Toni wasn't a suspect! Toni was our friend!

I started to shake my head at Tessa, but Toni said, "Oh, good, are you planning now to ask questions relating to a certain mystery? Because that is in reality the reason I invited you here today."

Tessa said, "Antonia Alfredo-Chin, who is that lady with the black hair who is not your grandmother, anyway?"

Toni nodded. "That is an easy question. This woman is a new housekeeper. She and my *abuelita* came to Washington from our nation together a couple of months ago. She is not very good at her job, and she does not smile. But why—?"

Tessa held up her hand. "If you don't mind, I am asking the questions here."

I closed my eyes and shook my head. Oh, Tessa.

But Toni giggled. "This is like a real detective show! What else do you want to know from me?"

"Why did your new housekeeper go to Mega Bird Farm this week to ask if Mr. Valenteen bought an ostrich egg there last week that he took to the National Museum of Natural History pretending to be from a delivery company that for real does not even *exist*?"

Toni looked at Tessa. Then she looked at Nate and me. "Huh?" she said.

Tessa said, "Okay, we can come back to that one. How about this? How well do you know this Mr. Valenteen guy from your nation? The one Hooligan knocked over on TV?"

Toni said, "Not well, but it is said he sometimes does

secret projects for my uncle, President Alfredo-Chin. It may be possible that he is a *spy*."

Nate and I looked at each other. *A spy?*

And Tessa said, "Aha! So when Mr. Valenteen took the ostrich egg to the museum—was that a special project for President Alfredo-Chin? Like a *spy* project?"

Toni didn't answer, but Nate nodded like he had just figured something out. "I see what you're getting at, Tessa! You think the idea was to embarrass Professor Bohn and Professor Rexington at their talk—make it seem like they're so dumb they can't tell the difference between an ostrich egg and a dinosaur egg. Then—if the professors were wrong and there was no dinosaur egg—the old legend could still be true, and President Alfredo-Chin could stay president in perpetuity!"

"Exactly," Tessa said, even though I know my sister, and I could tell she had never thought all that one bit.

Toni still didn't say anything. Instead, she got up and walked over to her rock collection. "I do not know about ostrich eggs, but I do know many people in my nation disbelieve that silly legend, and many people are in favor of democracy." She turned to face us. "That is why now, if you don't mind, I would like to show you something."

Toni's collection included a white geode, a purple amethyst, a lump of turquoise and two pieces of pyrite, also known as fool's gold. But the rock she brought over for us to look at wasn't pretty like those. It was gray and boring and oval-shaped. She held it out...

...and my heart almost stopped for the second time in an hour.

Tessa had turned pale, and her voice squeaked. "Is that what I think it is?"

"Yes," said Toni. "It is the missing dinosaur egg fossil from the National Museum."

CHAPTER TWENTY-SIX

Tessa's color came back fast.

"*Woot!* Cammie—get Mr. Morgan and Mr. Webb on the phone! The First Kids have solved another one! And Toni"—she looked at our friend sorrowfully—"I hate to tell you, but you are under arrest. Now—give over that dinosaur egg you stole!"

Tessa made a grab, which caused Toni to squeal and jump back.

"Oh, for gosh sake, Tessa, would you chill?" I said. "We are not arresting anybody. If Toni ever stole any egg, would she invite us over to see it?"

Tessa pouted. "Oh, *fine.* But, Toni, if you're not a thief, how did you get hold of a missing dinosaur egg?"

Toni shook her head. "I wish I knew. But the truth is it simply appeared in my rock collection."

Tessa crossed her arms over her chest again. "And when was that?"

"It was Thursday, one week ago. I had just said my prayers that night, and I looked up at my collection and saw it. I had seen the picture on Jan and Larry, so I knew immediately what it was."

I was scribbling as fast as I could and trying to think at the same time. Thursday was the same day the dinosaur egg's crate was scanned at the airport here in Washington, the same day Mr. Valenteen bought the ostrich egg at Mega Bird Farm and the same day Mr. Valenteen—pretending to be Red Heart Delivery—took the ostrich egg to the museum.

Just in case, I asked Toni if she had ever heard of Red Heart Delivery, and she said, "Yes! I saw a van with that name on our street. I noticed because I wondered if they only delivered flowers and chocolate and diamonds."

"When was that?" Tessa asked.

Toni frowned. "It was that same Thursday. I remember I was still wearing my clothes from horseback riding—and my lessons are on Thursday."

Tessa nodded. "So Mr. Valenteen must've replaced the dinosaur egg with an ostrich egg and brought the dinosaur egg here. After that, he must've brought it upstairs to put in Toni's collection."

Toni shook her head. "No, no—only the family and our guests may come upstairs in the residence! Mr. Valenteen would never be allowed."

"In that case, he gave it to somebody, and *they* brought it upstairs," Nate said. "But why? And who did he give it to?"

"It cannot have been my father," Toni said, "because he was away last week. But wait—I am forgetting.

There is the housekeeper, Mrs. Casera. She is permitted upstairs because of course she must do the cleaning."

"There you go," said Tessa. "I think Mr. Valenteen was working with Mrs. Casera, and he gave the egg to her."

I thought that might be right. "But why did she put it in Toni's rock collection?"

"And if Mrs. Casera was working with Mr. Valenteen," said Nate, "why did she have to go back to Mega Bird Farm to ask about the ostrich egg? There's something we're not getting here."

I thought of how Mrs. Casera and Toni's *abuelita* looked a little bit alike. "Toni," I said, "did Mr. Valenteen know your grandmother by sight? Or Mrs. Casera?"

Toni shrugged. "Perhaps not. As I told you, my abuelita does not like publicity, so she rarely appears on TV or in magazines."

"Then maybe," I said, thinking out loud, "Mr. Valenteen was supposed to give the egg to Mrs. Casera, and she was supposed to get rid of it—all to preserve the legend for President Alfredo-Chin. But instead, Mr. Valenteen gave the egg to your grandmother."

Toni said, "You mean it was a case of mistaken identity!"

I nodded. "And Mrs. Casera—when she didn't get the egg like she was supposed to—she went to Mega Bird Farm to check up."

"If you are right, it was my abuelita who put the egg in my rock collection," Toni said. "Maybe she did not know what it was, or maybe she did know and wanted a hiding place...."

Tessa jumped up. "Well, what are we waiting for? Let's go ask her!"

Toni remained seated. "If I may—there is something more important right now even than solving this mystery. You see, I asked you here today for a particular reason. I believe the First Kids are the only people in the world who can help me do what is right. We must return the dinosaur egg to its rightful owners at the museum, but we must do this without embarrassing my uncle, my father or anyone else from my nation. Is this possible? Will you help me?"

CHAPTER TWENTY-SEVEN

Nate and I looked at each other. We wanted to help—but how?

Tessa's reaction was different. She sat back down, rubbed her hands together and said: "*No problemo!* All we have to do is think sneaky. And thinking sneaky is one of my talents."

Nate nodded. "True."

And the way it turned out—Tessa was right. After about five minutes of brainstorming, she had added up one dinosaur egg, one Easter basket and one big Monday event at the White House to equal one foolproof plan.

"All we need now," she said in conclusion, "is chocolate chips."

Toni nodded. "There are plenty in the kitchen. But we must hurry! Your grandmother will be back in only one hour."

The kitchen in the residence part of the embassy is on the first floor and not that different from one in a normal house. When we walked in—luckily—no one was there. Toni went straight to a pantry cupboard and pulled out the chocolate chips. From another cupboard, she got a pan.

Then she poured the chips into the pan and turned on the stove.

"You've got to stir it, or they'll burn," I said.

"Who cares?" Tessa said. "It's not like anybody's going to eat it—*owieee!* Think of your teeth!"

"No, no one's going to eat it—but burnt chocolate smells terrible," I said. "Someone might come to investigate."

"Investigate what?" said a voice from the doorway— Toni's abuelita!

Now we had a puzzle. Did we tell her what we were doing? Ask her about the dinosaur egg—whether she had put it in Toni's collection, whether she knew what it was?

But what if she tried to stop us from returning it to Dr. Bohn and Dr. Rexington at the museum?

For a moment, we all froze. Then Toni turned and said—a little too cheerfully—"*Hello, Abuelita!* Uh...we were just making some, uh—"

"Easter treats!" My sneaky sister helped her out, and—without us kids even talking about it—the decision was made.

Abuelita raised her eyebrows. "Oh, yes? That is very nice."

"Abuelita," Toni said, thinking fast, "would you mind getting the beautiful Easter basket brought to me this afternoon by my friends? Only...I am sorry, but I am not sure where I put it. Perhaps in the parlor? Or my bedroom?"

Abuelita said certainly, she didn't mind looking, and was barely out the door when the three of us rushed to the stove. The chocolate had melted by now. It was smooth and glossy and smelled delicious—but we couldn't get sidetracked with a taste test. We had dipping to do.

It might be that someday you'll have to dip a dinosaur egg fossil in chocolate to disguise it, and if so, I have some advice:

1) Use tongs.
2) Dip repeatedly.
3) Have plenty of paper towels handy.
4) Decorate with sprinkles.

By the time Toni's grandmother found the Easter basket, our Easter egg of unusual size was chilling in the freezer, and—if I do say so myself—for a rock, it looked good. We thanked Toni's grandmother, then took the beautiful basket apart—which seemed a little sad. The nice chocolate eggs and cookies we put in a bowl for Toni's family. The Easter grass and a few jelly beans we left.

Later we would put our special chocolate egg in the center and walk right out of the embassy with it.

At least, that was the plan.

"And the Easter treats you made, may I see?" Abuelita asked.

Uh-oh.

I was worried, but Toni went straight over to the
freezer and opened it. Would the disguise be successful?

Abuelita studied the egg. Then she looked at
us...and for a split second, I was terrified she knew
exactly what we were up to. But she couldn't, could
she?

Still, it was a relief when she smiled and said, "Such
a large piece of chocolate!"

Score! So far, Tessa's sneaky plan was working
perfectly!

CHAPTER TWENTY-EIGHT

While the chocolate-dipped dinosaur egg finished cooling, Toni, Tessa, Nate and I went out and played Frisbee with the dogs. It was almost time for Granny to pick us up when we went back inside and packed the egg into the basket.

We were admiring our work when Abuelita came into the kitchen to say the White House van was out front.

That was when I thought of those unsmiling soldiers at the gate and realized maybe this wouldn't be so easy. None of us had ever tried to sneak a dinosaur egg fossil out of an embassy before. We didn't know what it would be like.

In the front hall, Abuelita gave us each a hug good-bye.

Then, with Tessa in the lead, Toni, Nate and I walked out the front door and around to the courtyard. At the same time, a woman from the embassy staff brought

Hooligan from the back. Since I was carrying the Easter basket, Nate took Hooligan's leash.

Through the black metal fence, I saw the White House van parked on the street. Also outside were two Secret Service guys. Jeremy was one, and I didn't know the other.

"Good-bye, dear friends." Toni gave us each a kiss on the cheek. When it was my turn she whispered, "And good luck!"

Toni is super pretty, and even though I was busy worrying, I noticed that her kiss made Nate turn pink.

We started walking toward the gate, and the soldier on the left unlatched it. With the dinosaur egg inside, the Easter basket was heavy and awkward to carry. I felt like every step was an effort, but I kept my chin tilted up so I would look confident.

Step, step, step, step, step. We were almost out...

...but then, in an instant, everything changed. The soldier on the left—responding to something he heard on the earpiece of his radio—shoved the metal gate shut—*clank!*—and now our way was blocked.

I froze. Outside the fence, Jeremy and the other Secret Service agent squared their shoulders and rocked back on their heels, ready for anything. Meanwhile, Malik emerged from the White House van.

Toni spoke to the soldier: "What is wrong? Open the gate at once!"

The soldier answered, "Your friends may leave, Miss Alfredo-Chin. But the holiday basket must remain."

Toni stamped her foot. "The basket is my gift to them!"

"I have my orders," he said. "Once the basket has been returned to Mrs. Casera, then your friends may leave."

Mrs. Casera—wha...? But then I smelled her cigarette smoke and turned. Out of nowhere, she had appeared beside me. Scowling, she reached for the Easter basket.

I have never been so scared, and—in case you don't know—I am not a brave person. But the egg was important to science, it didn't belong to her and—darn it—we had gone to a lot of trouble to get it back.

So instead of handing it over, I held it closer, stepped away and shook my head no.

Hooligan growled.

For a few seconds, it looked like a standoff—our team vs their team. The numbers were about equal, but their soldiers had way bigger guns.

Then Abuelita appeared in the courtyard. "Let the children pass, Sergeant."

"We have our orders, ma'am," he said.

"Orders?" she repeated. "From whom are these orders? I am the mother of the president of our nation and the mother of the ambassador!"

The soldier looked uncertain until Mrs. Casera spoke up. "His orders are from me."

"A *housekeeper*?" Abuelita said.

Mrs. Casera made an awful face she probably

thought was a smile. "I'm afraid that was only a cover. I am in fact a high official in the secret police force of our nation, sent here to ensure the security of the embassy."

Abuelita nodded. "Ah, I see. This explains why you are such a terrible housekeeper."

Mrs. Casera ignored the insult and grabbed the handle of the basket. To protect me, Hooligan lunged, which made Mrs. Casera shriek and let go, and after that things really got crazy. The sound of radio static and shouting voices filled the air. Ozzabelle showed up to yip and run in circles.

"Throw the basket over the fence, Cammie!" Tessa called, but the basket was way too heavy. Meanwhile, three men in suits, taking orders from Mrs. Casera, advanced toward me—and I was trapped!

It was Ozzabelle who came to my rescue, zigzagging between my feet and snapping at the men, who tried to stomp her with their shiny shoes. No way would Hooligan allow that! Protecting his little buddy, he jumped and threw his full furry weight against the first man, who fell against the second, who fell against the third, so that they all went over like dominoes.

Outside the fence, Jeremy was on his radio. Maybe Mom would send in the marines to rescue us! But if that got on the news, it would not look good for the friendship between the United States and a nearby nation.

My thoughts were as chaotic as the action around me, when all of a sudden, everything changed—like someone had hit the Pause button. First the soldiers at the gate turned their heads, then the three men in suits on the ground, then Abuelita and even the dogs.

They were looking at someone standing in one of the second-floor windows—and when finally Mrs. Casera looked up, too, she groaned in dismay.

The man in the window was wearing a blue work shirt. He had curly black hair, dark eyes, a crooked nose and a skinny face. His expression wasn't pouty like it is on his CDs, though. It was stern.

"Wait a second, that's—" I started to say, but Toni shushed me with a finger to her lips. When I looked again, the man was gone.

Tessa took advantage of the momentary confusion: "Run, Cammie!"

I did, and I could tell that now the soldiers didn't know what to do. Obey Abuelita? Obey Mrs. Casera?

Tessa crossed her arms over her chest and spoke to them: "It looks like you just have to decide for yourselves. Whose side are you on?"

CHAPTER TWENTY-NINE

For a moment, the soldier on the left looked hopeless and confused, but then his face changed. He had made his decision.

"You'll pay for this, Sergeant!" cried Mrs. Casera as he unlatched the gate and let us through.

"Thanks very much, Sergeant!" said Tessa. Then she shoved me ahead, and Nate and Hooligan followed. Before I knew what was happening, Granny had hustled us into the White House van and Malik was gunning the motor.

"Are you okay?" Granny asked. "And wherever did you get such a huge chocolate egg for your Easter basket?"

"We're fine," I said, breathing for what seemed like the first time in a while.

"But we can't tell you about the egg, Granny," said Tessa.

"We promised," said Nate.

"Hmph," said Granny. "Perhaps we will discuss the

egg later. For now, though, I have to tell you Easter dinner will be delayed. There are a couple of gentlemen waiting in the Treaty Room to see you."

It was Mr. Morgan and Mr. Webb in the Treaty Room—I mean, in case you hadn't figured that out. Mom was there, too, making a special guest appearance. So was Charlotte.

"Hey, hi—how was Pittsburgh?" Tessa asked when we'd all sat down. "We have bad news, though," she went on. "Professor Bohn didn't do it."

Mr. Morgan nodded. "We know. We established that the first day. So right after we sent you the postcard, we left Pittsburgh to travel to a certain nearby nation."

"Wait, what?" I said. "Why didn't you tell us?"

Mr. Morgan looked at Mom, and Mom said, "I'm afraid their trip was top secret."

"Oh, *fine*," said Tessa. "So you knew about it and didn't tell us!"

"I'm sorry," Mom said, and that was all. One thing I'm finding out—when your mom is the president, there are a lot of things she can't tell you.

"I bet we know some things that you don't," Tessa said—and you could practically hear the *nyah-nyah-nyah* in her voice. "Like how the housekeeper is an officer in the police and Mr. Valenteen is a *spy*."

Mr. Morgan and Mr. Webb looked at each other. "How did *you*—"

Tessa waved her arms the way she does. "Never mind. And we've got another secret, too, so don't even bother asking where the dinosaur egg is now, because we won't tell you."

Mr. Morgan said, "You know where the dinosaur egg is?"

Mom looked equally surprised, which—I have to admit—kind of made me feel a little *nyah-nyah-nyah* myself.

Tessa said, "I never said we knew where the egg was."

And Nate said, "But if we did, we'd for sure turn it over to the scientists it belongs to, the ones who want to study it."

"And now we have some questions for *you*, Mr. Morgan and Mr. Webb." Tessa crossed her arms over her chest. "At the embassy today, there was a guy in the window, and when he showed up, it was like he was a rock star or something. All of a sudden, the soldiers didn't know who to listen to."

Nate started to say, "Wasn't the guy in the window Eb—"

But Mr. Webb put a finger to his lips, and Mom said, "It will be better for everyone if we don't name names. I will only say this. There is a hero of the protest movement in a certain nearby nation who is beloved by the people there. It is even possible he will one day be elected to office. It is also possible that, for his own safety, he must remain in hiding for now. Who knows? He may even be in hiding in his nation's embassy in the United States—protected by relatives of the current president."

All of a sudden, things started to make sense.

"If that's true," I said, "maybe President Manfred Alfredo-Chin sent a high official in the secret police to find this guy...and maybe she didn't do such a good job?"

Mom nodded. "Maybe."

"Wow." Tessa shook her head. "So sometimes politics are so complicated even people in the same family disagree with each other! I'm sure glad it's not like that here."

"Not in our family, at least," Mom said. "And now that you three are safe and sound, the important thing is the egg. It must be returned as quietly as possible. And it looks to me like the First Kids are on the case."

CHAPTER THIRTY

The morning of the Easter egg roll was clear and bright. The party started at nine-thirty with "the President's Own" United States Marine Band playing "Here Comes Peter Cottontail," and Hooligan—trying to look dignified—making an appearance on the Truman Balcony wearing pink-and-white bunny ears.

Later, singers and dancers performed, and authors and actors and senators read stories. Nate played the piano—a song called "Easter Parade" by a man named Irving Berlin.

Meanwhile, Tessa and I got to roll Easter eggs with kids. I like the really little kids best because they don't understand we're supposed to be famous, and they just act normal.

All the time, though, what Tessa, Nate and I were really looking forward to was meeting one special guest, Professor Cordell Bohn.

We had an Easter basket to give him.

With all those people, we couldn't count on running

into Professor Bohn, so we made arrangements to meet him near the East Gate at noon.

"There he is." Tessa pointed. Nate was carrying the basket. I waved, and Professor Bohn waved back. When we got closer, I saw that his usually merry face looked sad.

"I have to go back to Pittsburgh tomorrow," he said. "It's been a tough time here in Washington. I don't think Professor Rexington is ever going to forgive me for letting the dinosaur egg get away."

Tessa consulted her Barbie watch, the one she's too old for. "In about thirty seconds," she said, "you are going to feel a whole lot better. But first I have one question. How come you called Jan and Larry to tell them the egg was missing? To certain people I won't name, that looked suspicious."

Professor Bohn raised his eyebrows. "I called because I wanted to get the word out," he said. "I thought if it was on the news, a lot of people would hear about it and someone might call the police with a tip. But"—he looked at each of us in turn—"I don't get it. *Why* am I going to feel better?"

"Because we have a present for you." Nate held out the basket.

Professor Bohn started to say, "Aw, you didn't have to—" but then he wasn't expecting the basket to be so heavy and almost dropped it on his foot. "What in the world...?"

"Don't try to eat that egg," Tessa warned him. "Seriously."

The oversized chocolate egg nestled among the jelly beans in the green Easter grass. We had asked the White House pastry chef to add a few pastel frosting flowers that morning, so the egg really did look nice.

Professor Bohn stared down at it, and his jaw dropped. "It's the right size, the right shape, the right weight, but...it can't be!"

"Yeah, it can," Tessa said.

"But this is wonderful!" Professor Bohn said. "I must contact the museum at once. They'll want to make an announcement, and—"

Tessa crossed her arms over her chest. Nate shook his head. My voice was stern: "No, no, no, no, *no*."

"We never gave this to you," Nate said.

"It just appeared, you don't know how," said Tessa. "It's a matter of national security."

"But still—good luck with your research," I said.

"And"—Tessa wagged her finger—"be sure to share with Professor Rexington! Even though you think she's wrong about how the dinosaur's related to the birds and all, scientists have to play fair just like everybody else."

THE WHITE HOUSE EASTER EGG ROLL

First Kid Tessa Parks can be forgiven for thinking an eggroll is something you eat at a Chinese restaurant. An eggroll really is a Chinese-style appetizer. Less well known is an egg roll—two words—a game in which competitors use a serving spoon to push eggs across a lawn. The tradition of egg rolling around Eastertime comes from England and is still popular in some places there.

With one exception, egg rolling is not so common in the United States. But that exception is a big one: the White House Easter Egg Roll, which takes place the Monday after Easter.

HISTORY

While some people say it was First Lady Dolley Madison who started the egg roll tradition in Washington, there is no proof of this. In fact, the first recorded egg-rolling activities there seem to have been spontaneous. After the Civil War, children enjoyed rolling hard-boiled eggs from their lunch pails on the slopes outside the Capitol in the spring. The local newspapers wrote about this, also noting approvingly that these children playing together were from all races and classes.

That kind of integration was unusual in nineteenth-century Washington. As a side note, you would have to fast-forward all the way to 1953, when Mamie Eisenhower was First Lady, before African-American children would be invited to attend the official Easter Egg Roll at the White House. More than fifty years after that, President and Mrs. Obama made a point of including same-sex couples and their children on the guest list.

The Easter tradition moved to the White House in 1878. That spring, Congress had outlawed games of any kind on the Capitol grounds to save the lawn. President Rutherford B. Hayes learned how disappointed local children were one evening when he was taking a walk. According to Hayes's journal, a boy approached him and shouted, "Say! Say! Are you going to let us roll eggs in your yard?"

The surprised president was from Ohio and didn't know about the local tradition. When his staff explained, he and his wife, Lucy, decided that yes, they would let the boy—and all the other children of the town—roll eggs on the White House lawn. Thus the White House Easter Egg Roll was born.

BUSINESS OPPORTUNITIES

By 1889, when Benjamin Harrison was president, the event was so well established that vendors selling fruit, waffles, peanuts, balloons, pinwheels and sweets set up shop outside the White House gates to serve the people waiting in line.

The vendors weren't the only ones who saw the egg roll as a business opportunity. Since adults were not allowed to attend without children, clever kids figured out they could get paid for escorting childless adults. Once on the grounds, the children doubled back to wait for their next customer. During the Great Depression of the 1930s, an eleven-year-old boy told a reporter the five quarters he earned that day would help pay his family's rent.

THE TROUBLE WITH EGGS

While the Easter Egg Roll has always been a hit with kids, it has not always been popular with the First Family. President Theodore Roosevelt's wife, Edith, wanted to call it off entirely because it was hard on the lawn and she didn't like the smell of leftover eggs. First Lady Pat Nixon had the same problem when she tried using hard-boiled eggs for an old-fashioned Easter egg hunt. The eggs that weren't found remained rotting outside for days—*pew!*

President Gerald Ford tried using plastic eggs, but it was President and Mrs. Ronald Reagan who came up with the most enduring solution: painted wooden eggs. Now thousands of colorful wooden eggs, stamped with the president's and First Lady's signatures, are given away every year as keepsakes.

Mrs. Reagan can claim an additional egg roll distinction. She not only hosted the event when her husband was president in the 1980s, but she also attended as a guest of President and Mrs. Calvin Coolidge when she was a child during the 1920s.

PRESIDENTIAL PETS

As a guest in 1927, the future First Lady might have seen the glamorous Grace Coolidge parading among the partygoers, carrying one of the best-known White House pets, Rebecca Raccoon. At the 1922 event, President Warren G. Harding's photogenic Airedale, Laddie Boy, sniffed kids, shook hands and did tricks. Eleanor Roosevelt brought first dogs Meggie, a Scottie, and Major, a German shepherd, to the 1933 egg roll.

Like the fictional Hooligan in *The Case of the Missing Dinosaur Egg*, the Obamas' Portuguese water dog, Bo, has appeared wearing pink-and-white bunny ears—and looking slightly embarrassed. Since the Nixon administration in the 1970s, the Easter Bunny himself has also stopped in, usually played by a White House staff member.

THE EGG ROLL TODAY

Today, in spite of the name, egg rolling is only a small part of what goes on at the annual event, which attracts about 35,000 people. Activities may include basketball, tennis and yoga, as well as cooking demonstrations and storytelling by celebrities. In recent years, J. K. Rowling has read from her Harry Potter books, President Barack Obama has read *Where the Wild Things Are* by Maurice Sendak, and actress Reese Witherspoon has read *The Best Pet of All* by David LaRochelle.

Among recent performers are Justin Bieber, Fergie, and the cast of *Glee*. On hand since 1889 has been "The President's Own" United States Marine Band, whose repertoire includes a John Philip Sousa song called "Easter Monday on the White House Lawn."

Most of the guests at the White House Easter Egg Roll get tickets through a free lottery conducted online. If you want to try your luck, go to www.recreation.gov to sign up a few weeks before Easter, usually early in March. In 2012, about one in eight people who wanted tickets got them. To keep the crowds manageable, guests are assigned a time slot and permitted to stay only about ninety minutes.

If you want more information on the White House Easter Egg Roll today, a good source is www.whitehouse.gov. For more on the event's history, check out a great article by C. L. Arbelbide in the spring 2000 *Prologue*, a publication of the National Archives, "With Easter Monday, You Get Egg Roll at the White House." It is also available online at www.archives.gov.